EASY PIANO

MORE
SIMPLE SONGS

THE EASIEST
EASY PIANO SONGS

T0066489

ISBN 978-1-4950-6912-3

HAL•LEONARD®
CORPORATION
7777 W. BLUEMOUND RD. P.O. BOX 13819 MILWAUKEE, WI 53213

Visit Hal Leonard Online at
www.halleonard.com

ALL OF ME

Words and Music by JOHN STEPHENS
and TOBY GAD

Moderately, with feeling

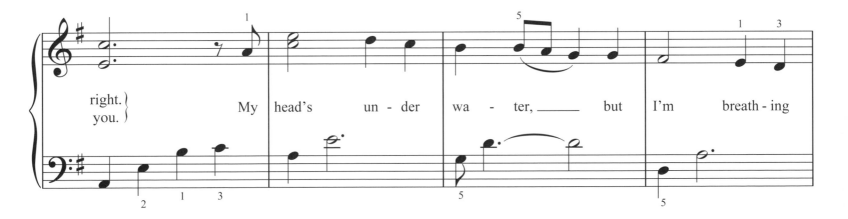

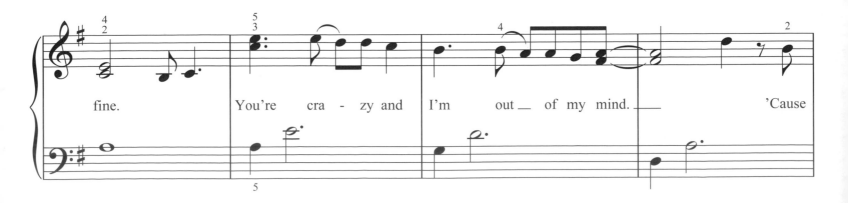

all   of me____   loves   all   of you.____   Love your

curves and all your edg - es,   all your   per - fect im - per - fec - tions.   Give your

all   to me,____   I'll give my   all   to you.____   You're my

end and my be - gin - ning.   E - ven   when I lose, I'm win -

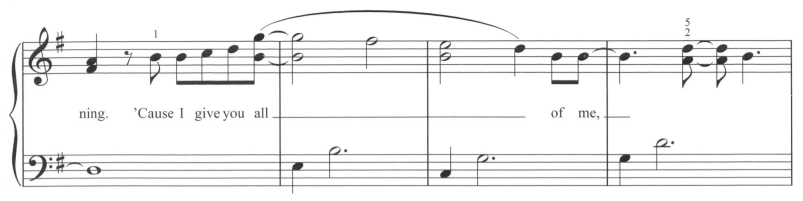

ning.   'Cause I give you all _____ of me, _____

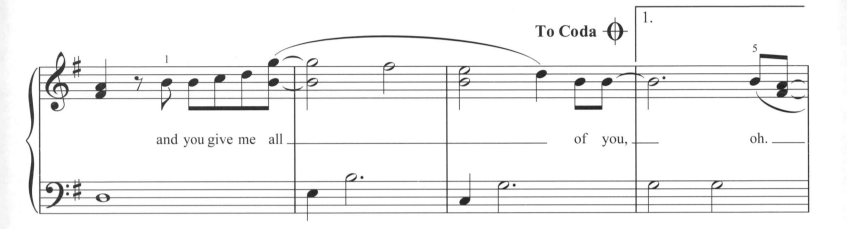

To Coda ⊕ |1.

and you give me all _____ of you, __ oh. __

|2.

__ __ oh. __ Give me all __ of   you. _____

Cards   on the ta - ble, __ we're __ both show - ing __ hearts.

D.S. al Coda

Risk - ing it all, though _ it's _ hard. 'Cause

CODA

I give you all _

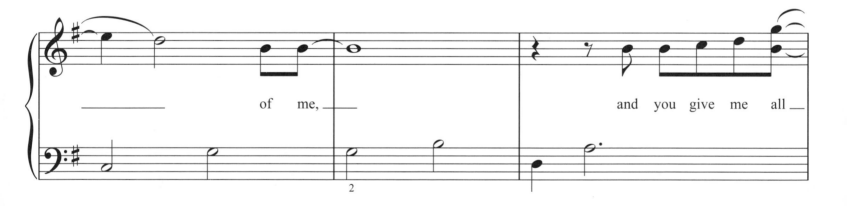

of me, _ and you give me all _

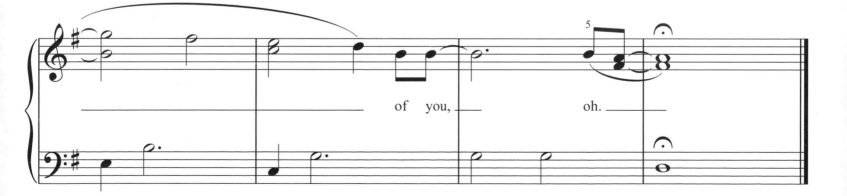

of you, _ oh. _

ANY DREAM WILL DO

from JOSEPH AND THE AMAZING TECHNICOLOR® DREAMCOAT

Music by ANDREW LLOYD WEBBER
Lyrics by TIM RICE

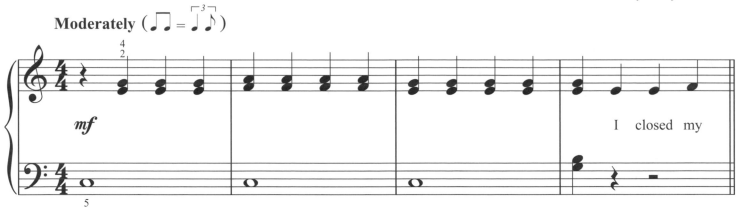

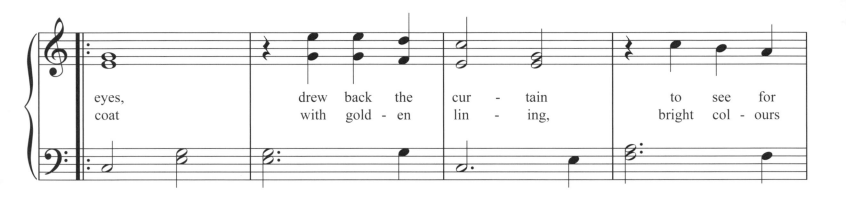

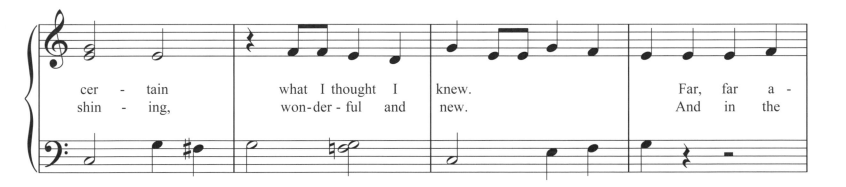

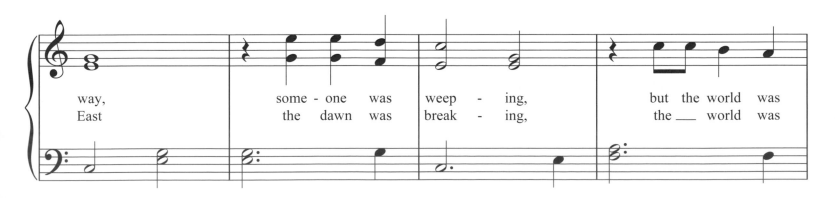

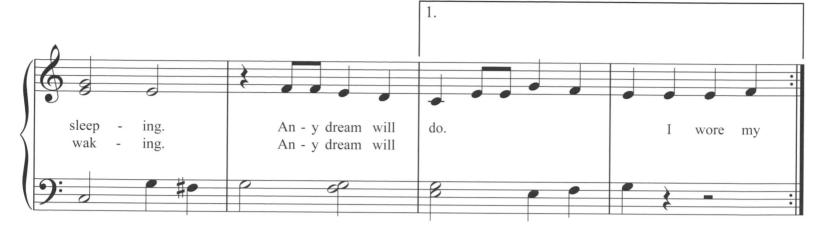

sleep - ing.
wak - ing.
An - y dream will do.
An - y dream will

I wore my

do.

A crash of drums, __ a flash of light, __ my

gold - en coat flew out of sight, __ the col - ours fad - ed in - to dark - ness,

I was left a - lone.

May I re -

turn   to   the   be - gin - ning,   the   light   is   dim - ming

and   the dream   is,   too.   The   world   and   I,

we   are   still   wait - ing,   still   hes - i - tat - ing.   An - y dream will

do.   An - y dream will   do.

AMAZING GRACE

Words by JOHN NEWTON
Traditional American Melody

Slowly, with reverence

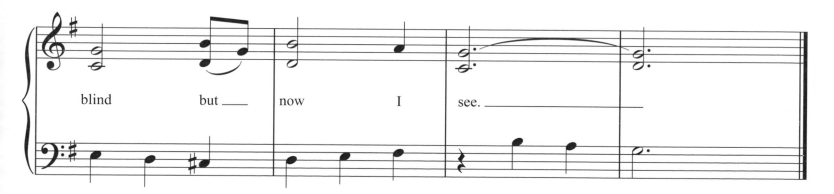

CHIM CHIM CHER-EE

from Walt Disney's MARY POPPINS

Words and Music by RICHARD M. SHERMAN
and ROBERT B. SHERMAN

Lightly, with gusto

Chim chim-in-ey, chim chim-in-ey, chim chim cher - ee! A
Up where _ the smoke is _ all bil - lered and curled 'tween
Chim chim-in-ey, chim chim-in-ey, chim chim cher - ee! When

sweep is as luck - y as luck - y can be.
pave - ment and stars is the chim - ney sweep world. When there's
you're with a sweep you're in glad com - pa - ny.

Chim chim-in-ey, chim chim-in-ey, chim chim cher-oo! Good
'ard - ly ___ no day ___ nor 'ard - ly no night, there's
No - where _ is there a more 'ap - pi - er crew than

To Coda ⊕

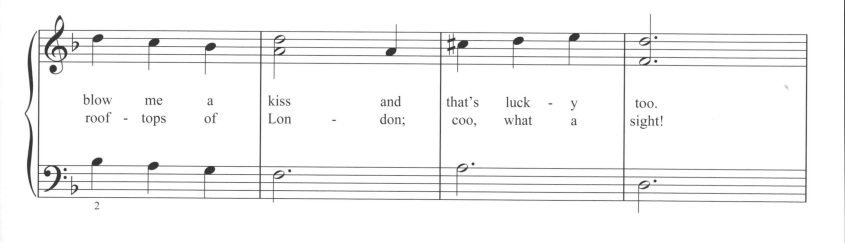

luck will rub off when I shake 'ands with you, or
things 'alf in shad - ow and 'alf - way in light, on the
them wot sings "chim chim cher - ee, chim cher - oo!"

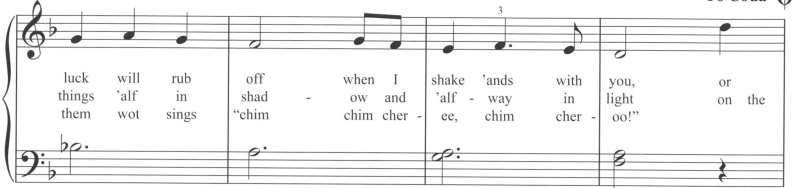

blow me a kiss and that's luck - y too.
roof - tops of Lon - don; coo, what a sight!

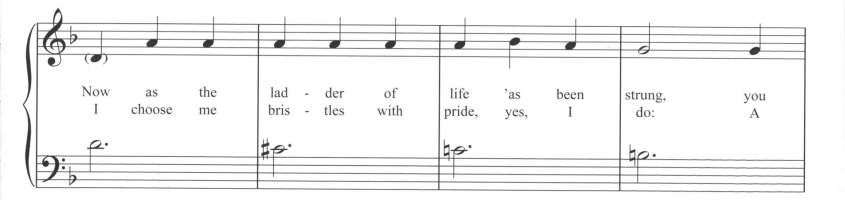

Now as the lad - der of life 'as been strung, you
I choose me bris - tles with pride, yes, I do: A

14

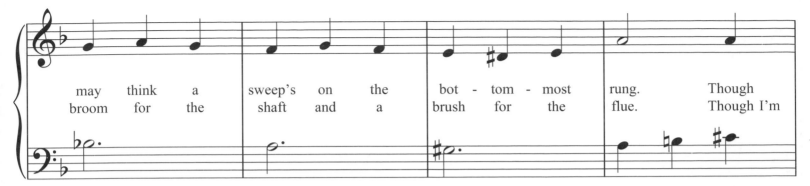

may think a | sweep's on the | bot - tom - most | rung. Though
broom for the | shaft and a | brush for the | flue. Though I'm

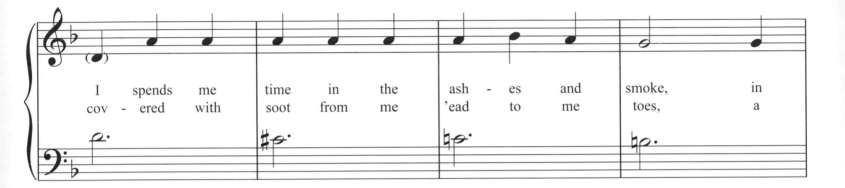

I spends me | time in the | ash - es and | smoke, in
cov - ered with | soot from me | 'ead to me | toes, a

1st time: D.C.
2nd time: D.C. al Coda

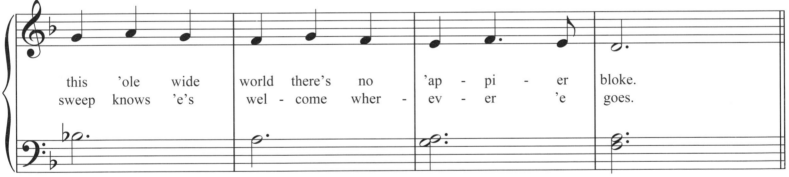

this 'ole wide | world there's no | 'ap - pi - er | bloke.
sweep knows 'e's | wel - come wher - | ev - er 'e | goes.

CODA

Chim chim - in - ey | chim chim, cher - ee, | chim cher - oo!

BELLA'S LULLABY
from the Summit Entertainment film TWILIGHT

By CARTER BURWELL

BRAVE

Words and Music by SARA BAREILLES
and JACK ANTONOFF

Moderately

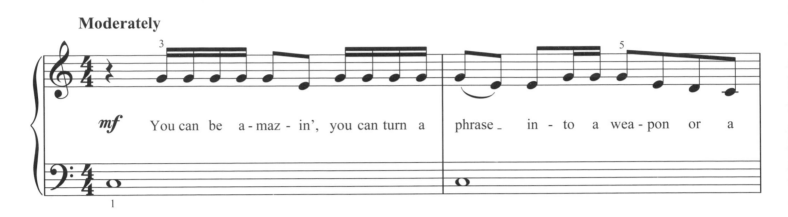

You can be a-maz-in', you can turn a phrase _ in-to a wea-pon or a

drug. You can be the out-cast _ or be the back-lash of some-bod-y's lack of

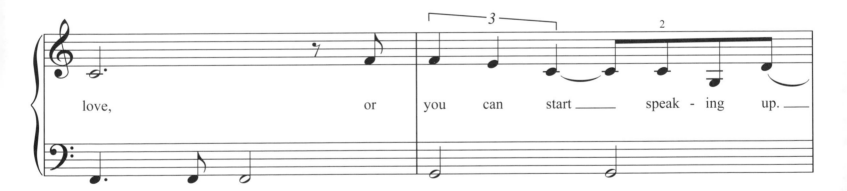

love, or you can start _ speak-ing up. _

Noth-in's gon-na hurt you _ the way that words do when they set-tle 'neath _ your

skin. Kept on the in - side and no sun - light some - times a shad - ow

wins. But I won - der what would hap - pen if you

say what you wan - na say and let the words fall out hon - est - ly.

I wan - na see you be brave ___ with what you wan - na say and let the words fall

out   hon - est - ly.   I   wan - na see you be   brave.___ Just wan - na see   you.

I   just wan - na see you.___ I   just wan - na see   you._____   I   wan - na see you be   brave.___

To Coda ⊕

___ Just wan - na see you.   I   just wan - na see you. __ I   just wan - na see   you,_____

I   wan - na see   you be   brave.

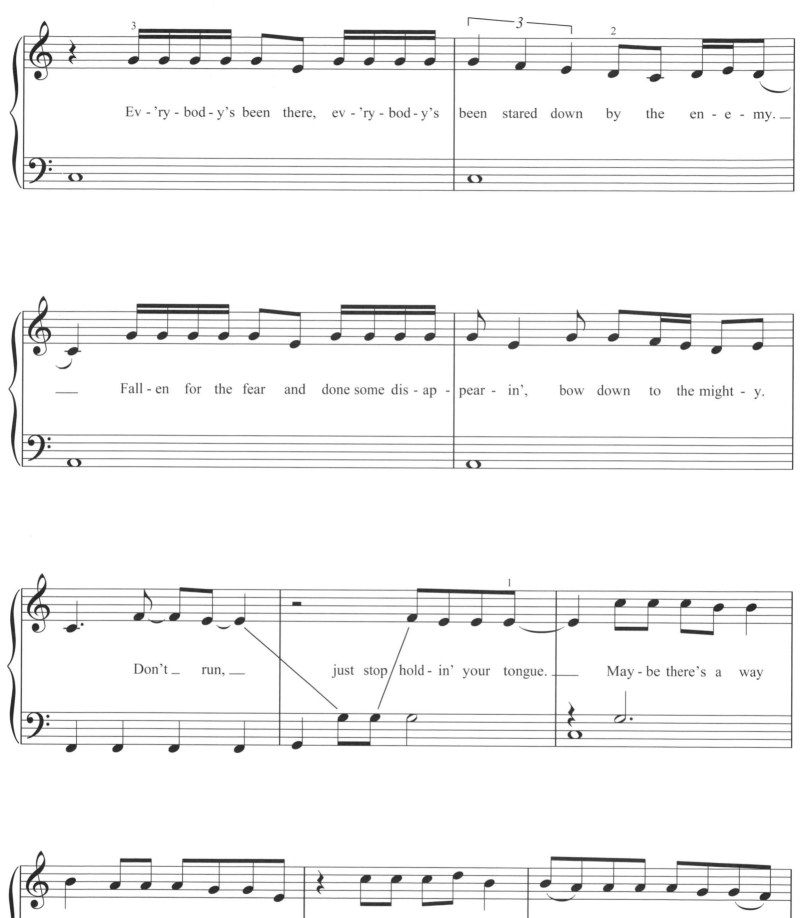

Ev-'ry-bod-y's been there, ev-'ry-bod-y's been stared down by the en-e-my. __

__ Fall-en for the fear and done some dis-ap-pear-in', bow down to the might-y.

Don't __ run, __ just stop hold-in' your tongue. __ May-be there's a way

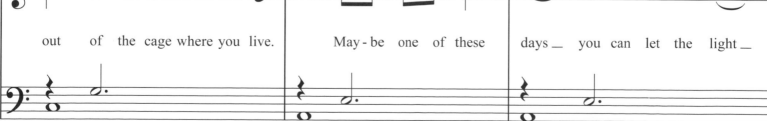

out of the cage where you live. May-be one of these days __ you can let the light __

in and show ___ me how big your brave ___ is. Say what you wan - na say

and let the words fall out hon - est - ly. I wan - na see you be brave ___

___ with what you wan - na say and let the words fall out hon - est - ly.

I wan - na see you be brave. ___ And ___ since your ___ his - to - ry of si - lence

won't do you an - y good,   did you think it would? ____   Let your words _ be

D.S. al Coda

an - y - thing but emp - ty.   Why don't you tell them the   truth? _____

CODA

just wan - na see you be,   I just wan - na see you.   I just wan - na see you.

I just wan - na see you. ____

1.

2.

BRIDGE OVER TROUBLED WATER

Words and Music by
PAUL SIMON

Moderately

When you're | wea - ry, ___ | feel - in'
down and out, ___ | when you're on the

small, | when tears are | in your
street, | when eve - ning falls | so

eyes,   I'll   dry   them _ all; ___
hard,   I   will   com-fort   you. ___

I'm   on   your   side.   Oh,   when   times _ get
I'll   take   your   part.   Oh,   when   dark - ness

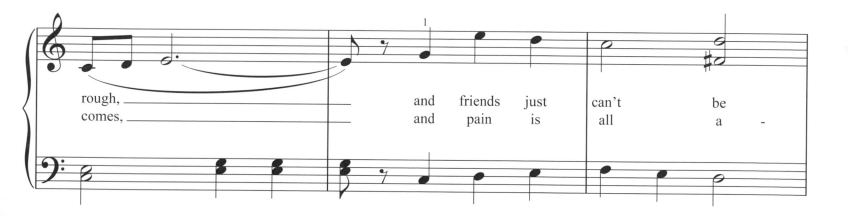

rough, ___   and   friends   just   can't   be
comes, ___   and   pain   is   all   a -

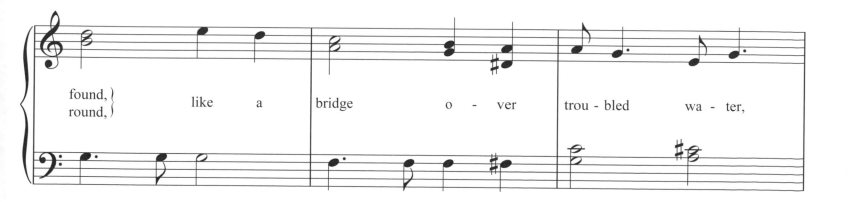

found, }
round, }   like   a   bridge   o - ver   trou - bled   wa - ter,

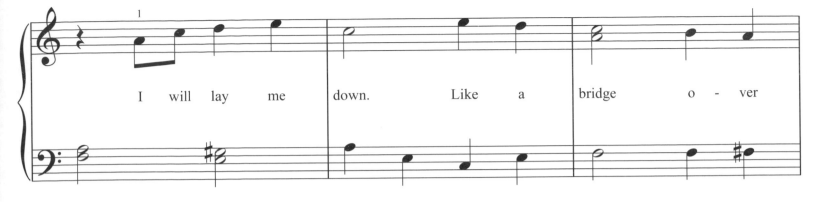

I will lay me down. Like a bridge o - ver

1.

trou - bled wa - ter, I will lay me down. _____

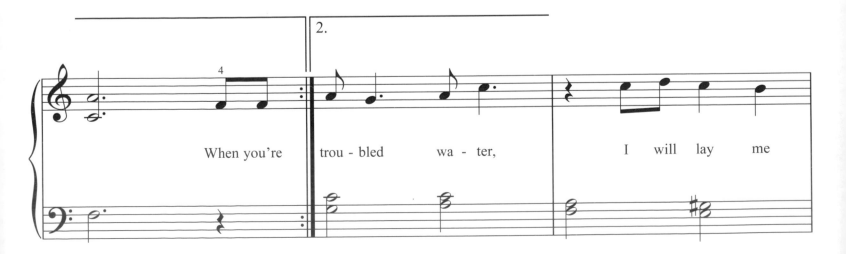

2.

When you're trou - bled wa - ter, I will lay me

down.

Sail on, sil - ver girl, sail on by.

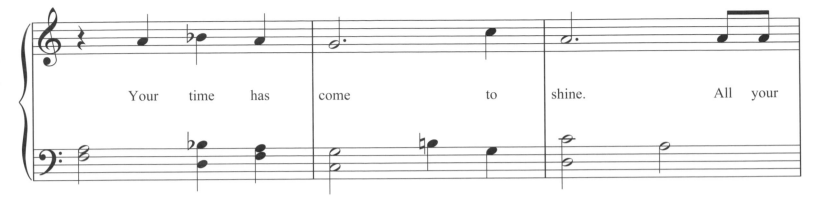

Your time has come to shine. All your

dreams are on their _ way. _____ See how they

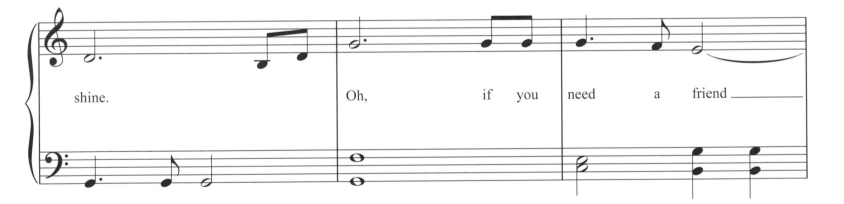

shine. Oh, if you need a friend _____

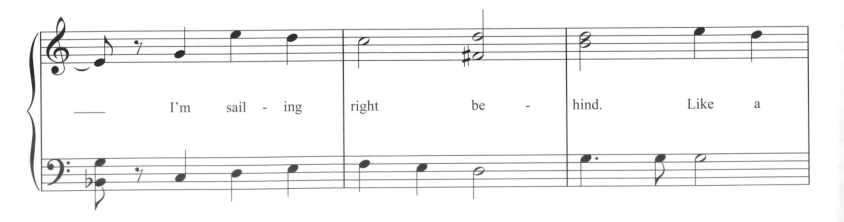

_____ I'm sail - ing right be - hind. Like a

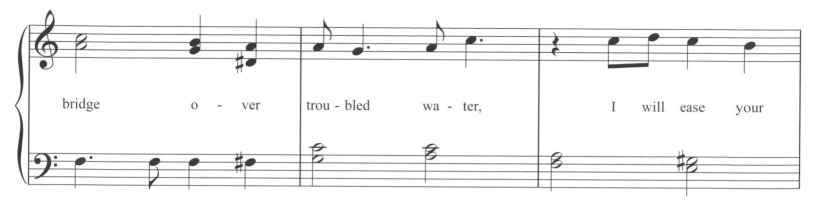

bridge   o - ver   trou - bled   wa - ter,   I   will   ease   your

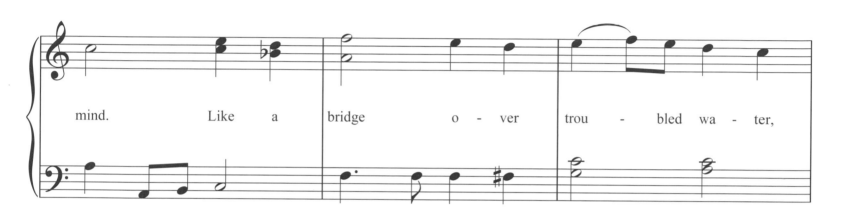

mind.   Like   a   bridge   o - ver   trou - bled wa - ter,

I   will   ease   your   mind.

rit.

CAN'T HELP FALLING IN LOVE

from the Paramount Picture BLUE HAWAII

Words and Music by GEORGE DAVID WEISS,
HUGO PERETTI and LUIGI CREATORE

Moderately slow

Wise men

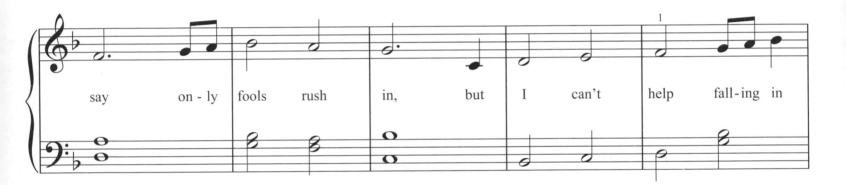

say on - ly fools rush in, but I can't help fall-ing in

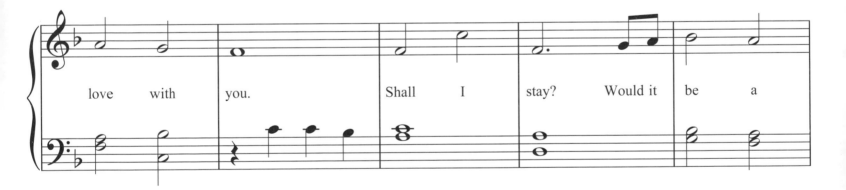

love with you. Shall I stay? Would it be a

sin if I can't help fall-ing in love with you?

Like a riv - er flows sure-ly to the sea; dar-ling, so it goes. Some things _ are meant to

be. Take my hand, take my whole life too. For

I can't help fall - ing in love with you. For

I can't help fall-ing in love with you. _____

CANDLE IN THE WIND

Words and Music by ELTON JOHN
and BERNIE TAUPIN

Good - bye, Nor - ma Jean. Though I nev - er
Lone - li - ness was tough, the tough - est role

knew you at all, _____ you had the grace to hold your - self _____ while
you ev - er played. _____ Hol - ly - wood cre - at - ed a su - per - star _____ and

those a - round_ you crawled. ___
pain was the price you paid. ___

They crawled out of the
And e - ven when you

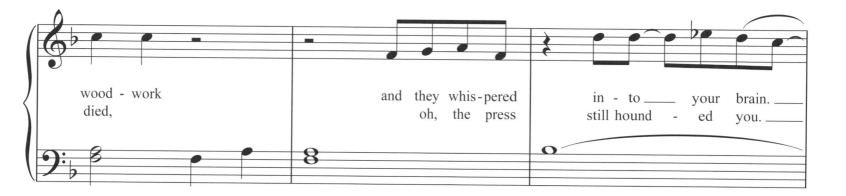

wood - work
died,

and they whis-pered
oh, the press

in - to ___ your brain. ___
still hound - ed you. ___

___ They set you ___ on a
___ All the pa - pers had

tread - mill
to say

and they
was they that

made you change_ your name. ___
Mar - i - lyn was found in the nude.

And it

seems to me ___ you lived your life ___ like a can - dle in ___ the

wind, nev - er know-ing who to cling to when the rain set in. ___

And I would have liked to've known you but I was just a

kid. Your can - dle burned out long ___ be - fore ___

your leg - end ev - er did. _____

Good - bye Nor - ma Jean. Though I nev - er

knew you ___ at all, _____ you had the grace to hold your - self _____ while

those a - round __ you crawled. __

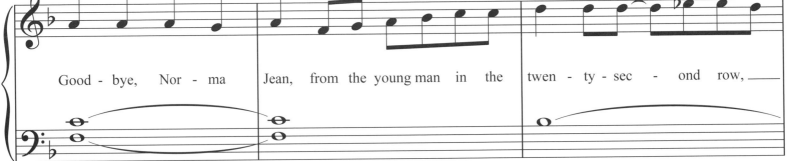

Good - bye, Nor - ma Jean, from the young man in the twen - ty - sec - ond row, __

__ who sees you as some - thing more than sex - ual, __ more than

D.S. al Coda

just our Mar - i - lyn Mon - roe. And it

CODA

I

would have liked to know you. Oh, ___ but I was just a kid, your

can - dle burned out long ___ be - fore ___ your

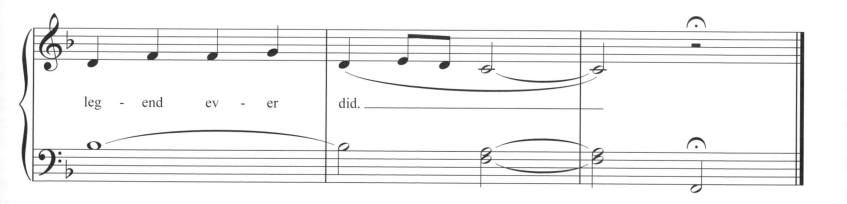

leg - end ev - er did. ___

CLOCKS

Words and Music by GUY BERRYMAN,
JON BUCKLAND, WILL CHAMPION
and CHRIS MARTIN

Moving along

The lights go out and I can't be saved, _ tides that I tried to
Con - fu - sion that nev - er stops, _ clos - ing walls and the

swim a - gainst _ have brought me down up - on my knees. _
tick - ing clocks. _ Gon - na come back and take you home. _ I

Oh, I beg, I beg and plead, _ sing - ing... come out with
could not stop that you now know, _ sing - ing... come out up -

things un - said. _ Shoot an ap - ple off my head. And a
on my seas, _ curse missed op - por tun - i - ties. _ Am I

trou - ble that can't be named, ___ a ti - ger's wait - ing
a part ___ of the cure? ___ Or am I a part of

to be tamed, ___ sing - ing...
this dis - ease, ___ sing - ing...

You ___

___ are.

You ___

___ are.

You ___

And noth - ing else com - pares. _____

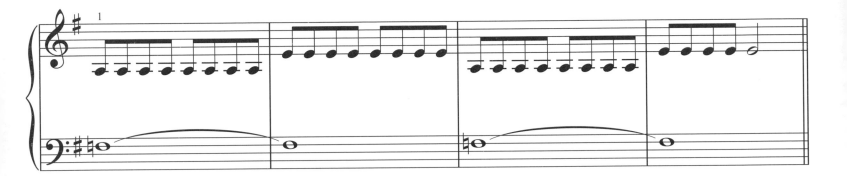

You _____ are.

Home, home, where I want- ed to

go. _p_

Repeat and Fade **Optional Ending**

COLOUR MY WORLD

Words and Music by
JAMES PANKOW

Slow Ballad

time goes on, _____ I re - al - ize

just what you mean _____ to _____

me. And now,

now that you're near, prom - ise your

love that I've wait - ed to share.

And dreams of our mo - ments to -

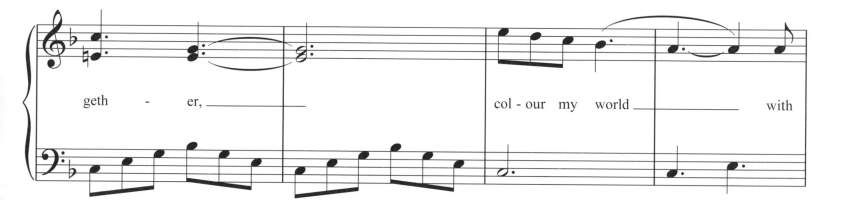

geth - er, col - our my world with

hopes of lov - ing you.
rit.

CRAZY

Words and Music by
WILLIE NELSON

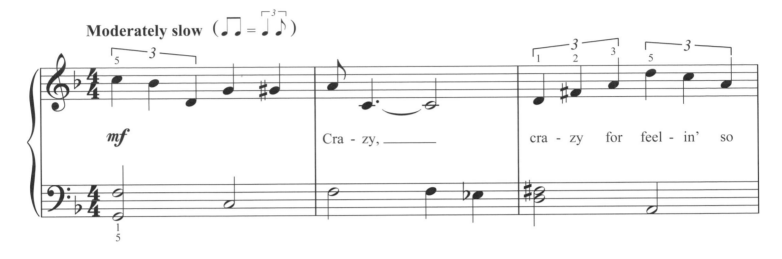

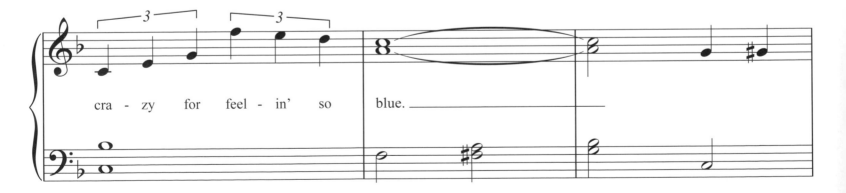

I know _____ you'd love me as long as you want - ed, _____

_____ and then some - day _____ you'd leave me for some - bod - y

new. _____ Wor - ry, _____

why do I let my - self wor - ry, _____

won - d'rin' _____ what in the world did I do? _____

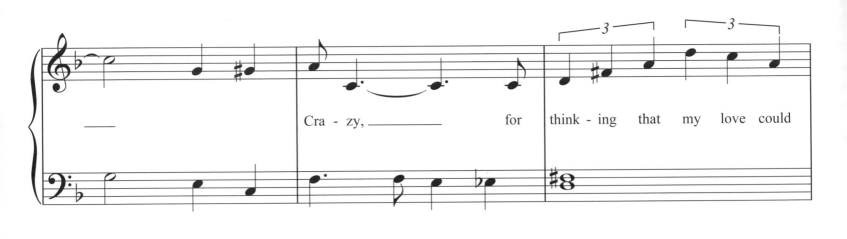

_____ Cra - zy, _____ for think - ing that my love could

hold you. _____ I'm cra - zy for try - in',

cra - zy for cry - in', and I'm cra - zy for lov - in' you!

rit.

DANNY BOY
(Londonderry Air)

Words by FREDERICK EDWARD WEATHERLY
Traditional Irish Folk Melody

Smoothly, with expression

Oh, Dan - ny Boy, the pipes, the pipes are
come and all the flow'rs are

call - ing, from glen to glen, and
dy - ing, if I am dead, as

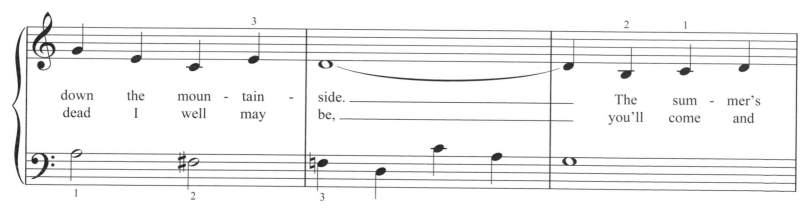

down the moun - tain - side. The sum - mer's
dead I well may be, you'll come and

52

gone   and   all   the   ros - es   fall   -   ing; _____
find   the   place   where   I   am   ly   -   ing, _____

_____ 'tis   you,   'tis   you   must   go   and   I   must
_____ and   kneel   and   say   an   A -   ve   there   for

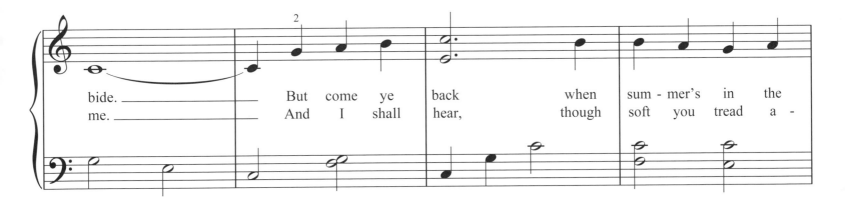

bide. _____   But   come   ye   back   when   sum - mer's   in   the
me. _____   And   I   shall   hear,   though   soft   you   tread   a -

mead   -   ow, _____   or   when   the   val   -   ley's
bove _____ me, _____   and   all   my   grave   will

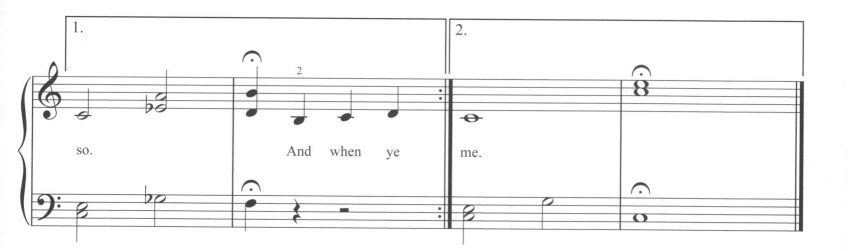

THE ENTERTAINER

By SCOTT JOPLIN

56

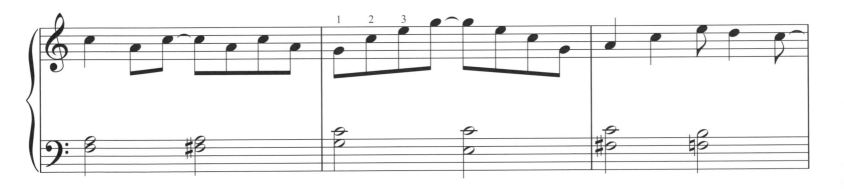

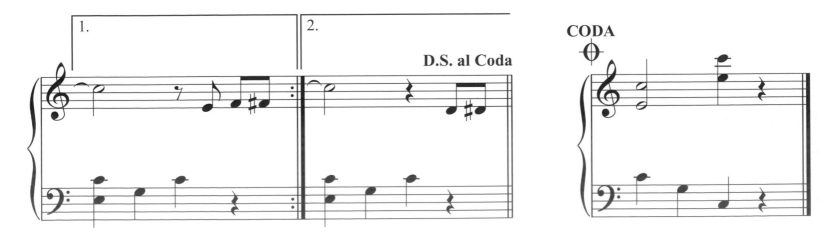

EASTER PARADE
from AS THOUSANDS CHEER

Words and Music by
IRVING BERLIN

Moderately

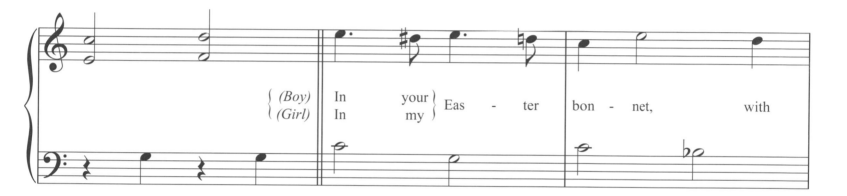

(Boy) In your
(Girl) In my } Eas - ter bon - net, with

all the frills up - on it, *you'll*
I'll } be the grand - est

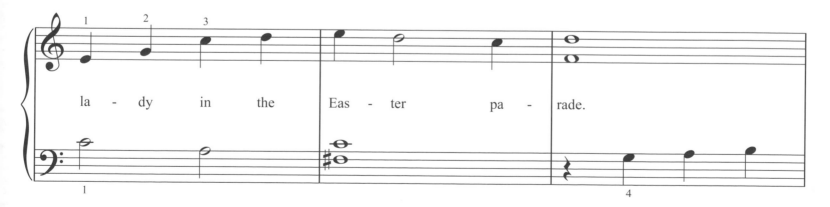

la - dy in the Eas - ter pa - rade.

58

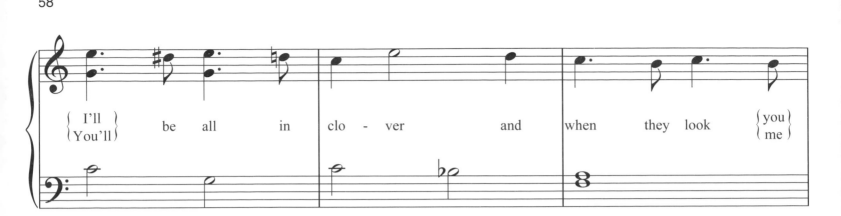

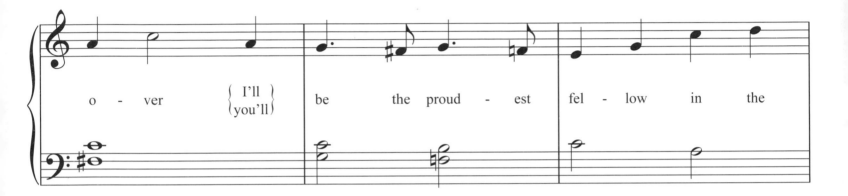

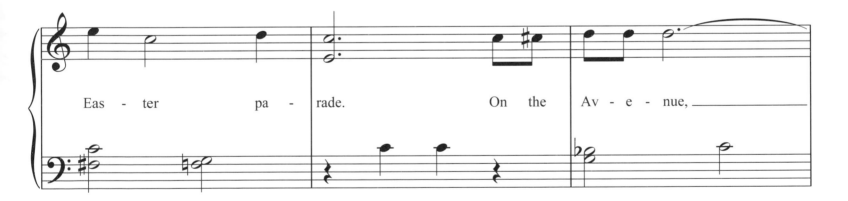

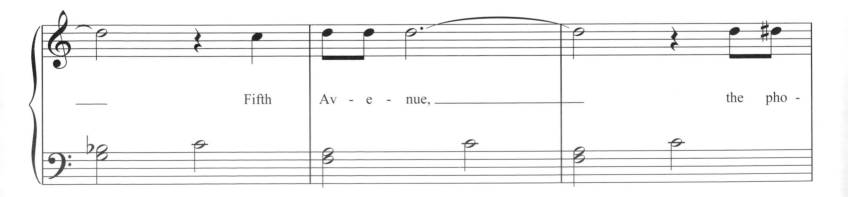

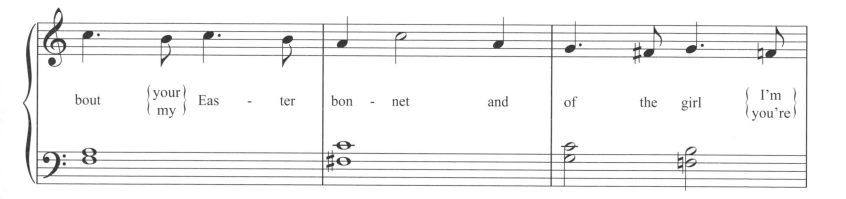

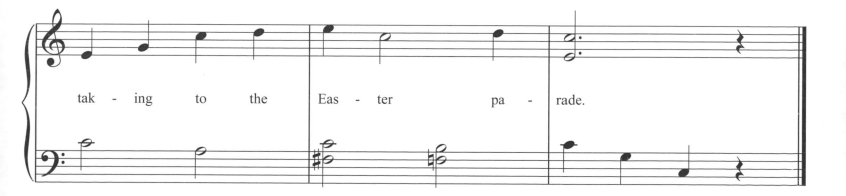

EDELWEISS
from THE SOUND OF MUSIC

Lyrics by OSCAR HAMMERSTEIN II
Music by RICHARD RODGERS

Slowly, with expression

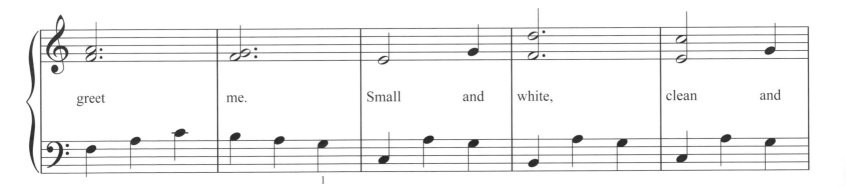

Blos - som of snow may you bloom and grow, bloom and

grow for - ev - er. E - del - weiss,

E - del - weiss, bless my home - land for - ev -

er. *rit.*

EVERYBODY WANTS TO RULE THE WORLD

Words and Music by IAN STANLEY,
ROLAND ORZABAL and CHRISTOPHER HUGHES

Moderately (straight 8ths)

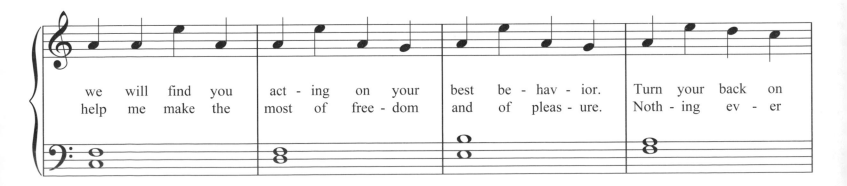

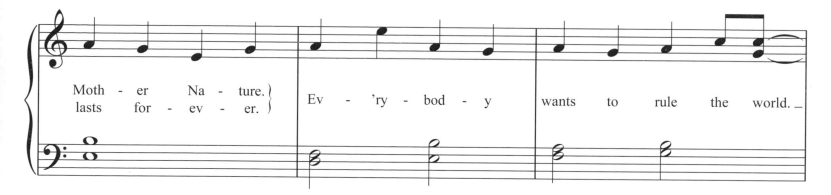

Moth - er Na - ture.}
lasts for - ev - er.} Ev - 'ry - bod - y wants to rule the world. _

1.

2.

There's a room where the

light won't find you hold - ing hands while the walls come tum - bling down. _

63

When they do, I'll be right be - hind you. So glad we've

al - most made it; so sad they had to fade it. Ev - 'ry - bod - y

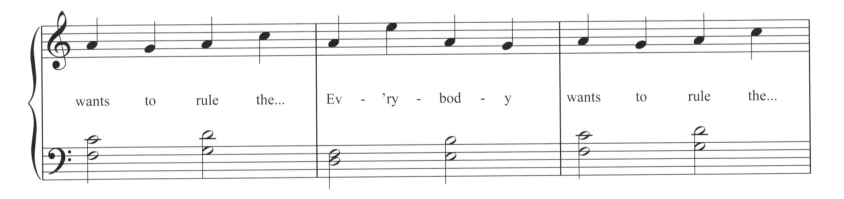

wants to rule the... Ev - 'ry - bod - y wants to rule the...

Ev - 'ry - bod - y wants to rule the world.

FAIRYTALE OPENING

from SHREK

Music by JOHN POWELL
and HARRY GREGSON-WILLIAMS

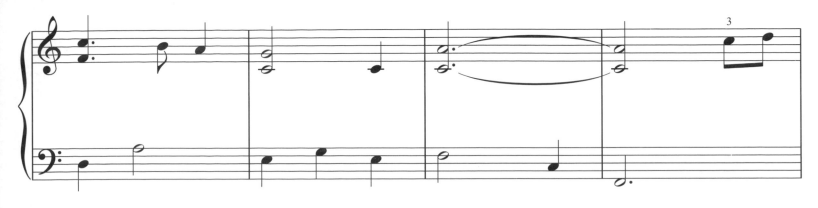

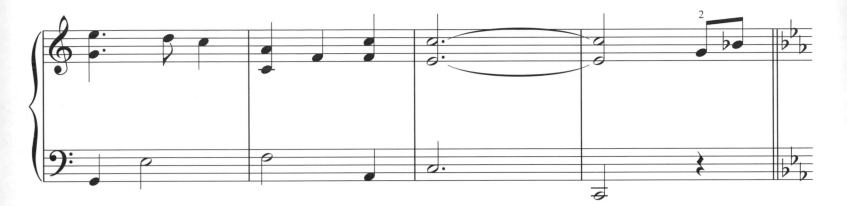

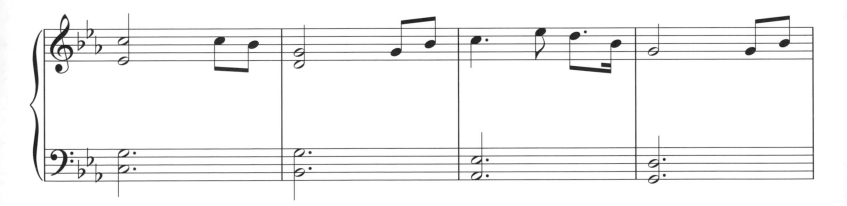

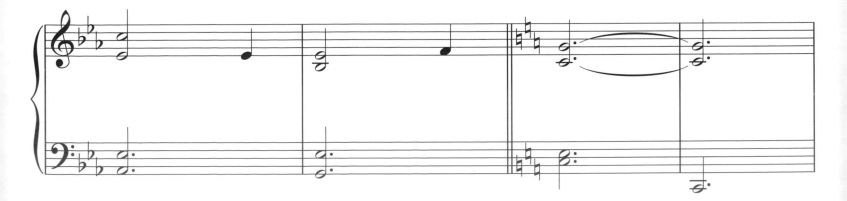

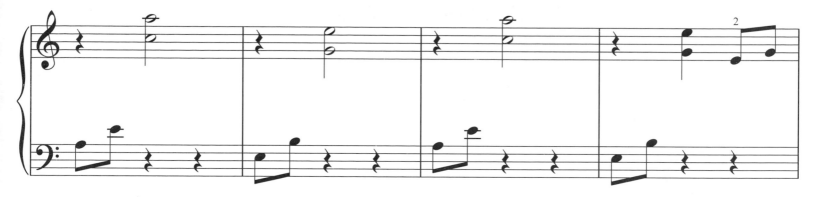

FOR GOOD
from the Broadway Musical WICKED

Music and Lyrics by
STEPHEN SCHWARTZ

Tenderly

Glinda: I've heard it said that peo - ple

be that we will

come in - to our lives for a rea - son, _____ bring - ing some - thing we must learn. And we are

nev - er meet a - gain in this life - time, _____ so let me say be - fore we part: So much of

led to those who | help us most to grow, if we | let them, _____ and we
me is made of | what I learned from you, you'll be | with me _____ like a

help them in re-turn. | Well, I don't know if I be-|lieve that's true, but I
hand-print on my heart. | And now what-ev-er way our | sto-ries end, I

know I'm who I am to-day be-|cause I knew you... _____ | Like a
know you have re-writ-ten mine by | be-ing my friend... _____ | Like a

com-et pulled from or-bit as it | pass-es a sun, __ like a | stream that meets a boul-der
ship blown from its moor-ing by a | wind off the sea, __ like a | seed dropped by a sky-bird

half-way through the wood, ___ who can say ___ if I've been changed for the bet - ter? But
in a dis - tant wood, ___ who can say ___ if I've been changed for the bet - ter? But

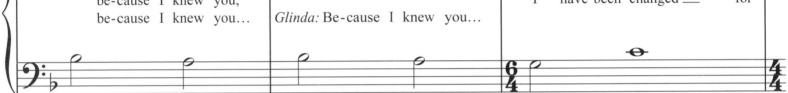

1.

be-cause I knew you,
be-cause I knew you... *Glinda:* Be-cause I knew you...

I have been changed ___ for

2.

good. *Elphaba:* It well may I have been changed for

good... *Elphaba:* And just to clear the air, ___ I ask for - give-ness for the things I've done you

blame me for. ___ *Glinda:* But then, I guess we know there's blame to share, _ *Both:* and

none of it seems to mat-ter an-y - more... ___ *Glinda:* Like a com-et pulled from or-bit as it

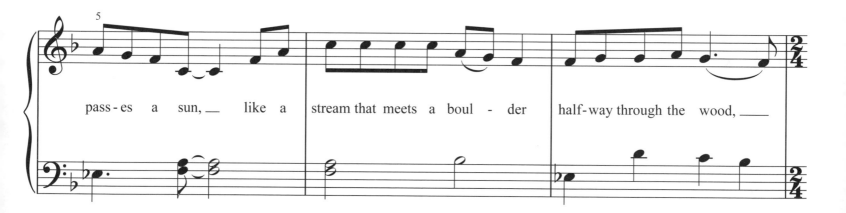

pass-es a sun, ___ like a stream that meets a boul - der half-way through the wood, ___

Both: who can say ___ if I've _ been changed for the bet - ter?

72

I do be-lieve I have been   changed for the   bet-ter..._____ *Glinda:* And

be-cause I knew you...   *Elphaba:* Be-cause I knew you...   *Both:* Be-cause I knew you...

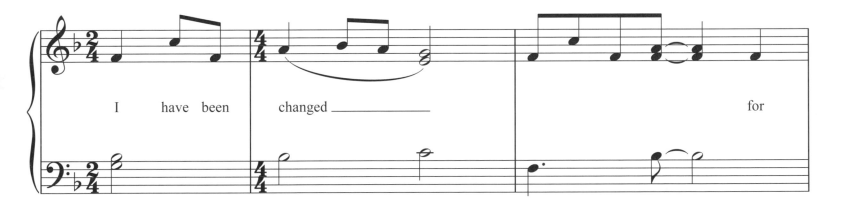

I have been   changed_____   for

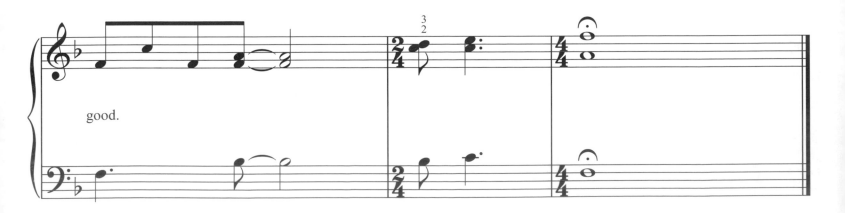

good.

GOD BLESS AMERICA®

Words and Music by
IRVING BERLIN

Moderately, in 2

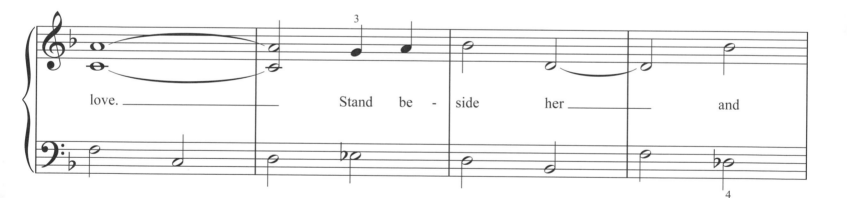

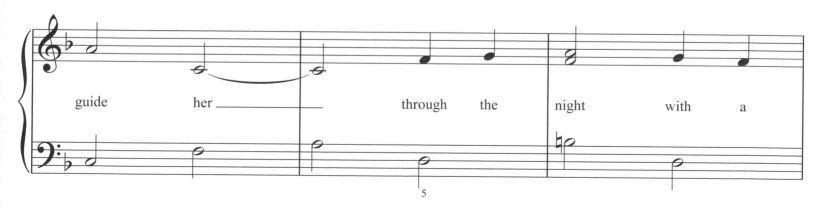

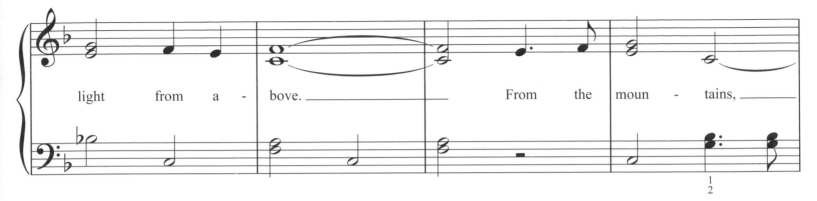

light   from   a - bove. _____   From   the   moun - tains, _____

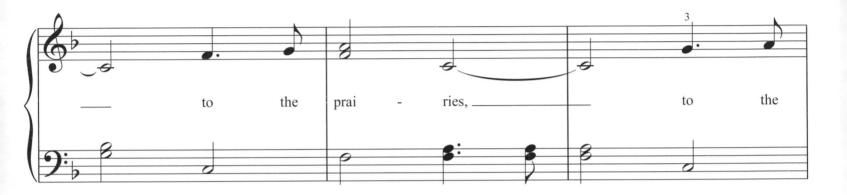

_____   to   the   prai - ries, _____   to   the

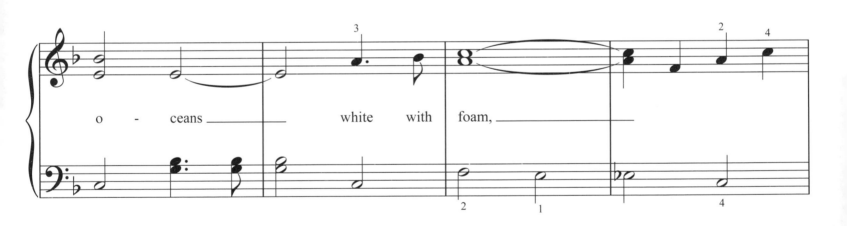

o - ceans _____   white   with   foam, _____

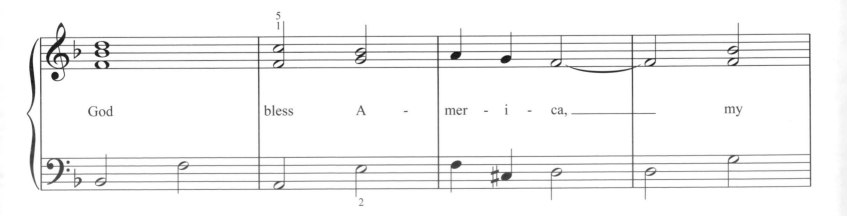

God   bless   A - mer - i - ca, _____   my

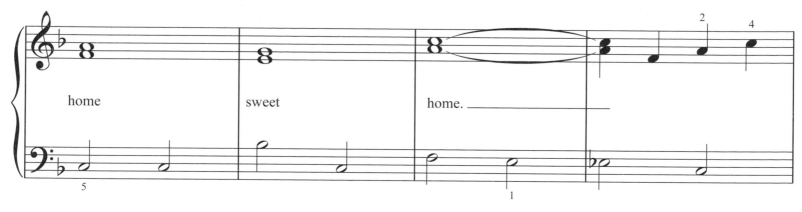

home sweet home.

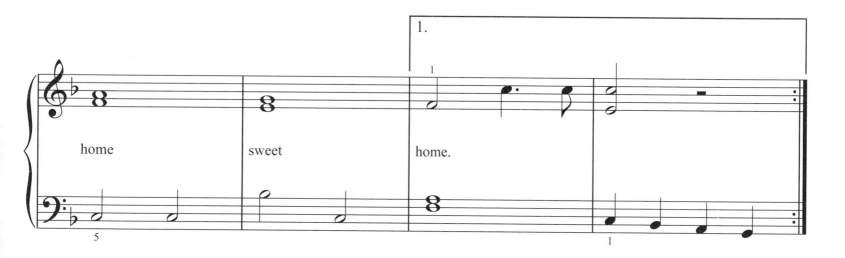

God bless A - mer - i - ca,   my

1.

home sweet home.

2.

home.   *molto rit.*

FORREST GUMP – MAIN TITLE
(Feather Theme)
from the Paramount Motion Picture FORREST GUMP

Music by ALAN SILVESTRI

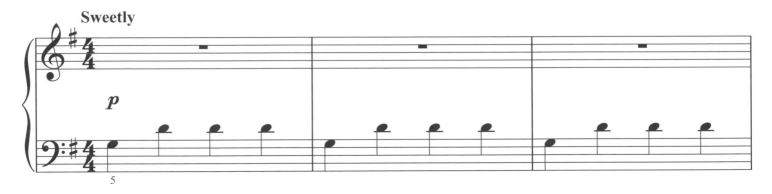

molto cresc.

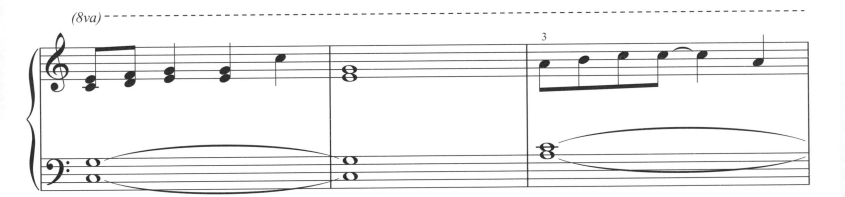

FÜR ELISE

By LUDWIG VAN BEETHOVEN

HALLELUJAH

Words and Music by
LEONARD COHEN

mi - nor fall, __ the ma - jor lift, __ the baf - fled king __ com - pos - ing __ Hal - le -

lu - jah. __ Hal - le - lu - jah, __ Hal - le -

lu - jah, __ Hal - le - lu - jah, __ Hal - le -

lu - jah.

8vb

HEART AND SOUL
from the Paramount Short Subject A SONG IS BORN

Words by FRANK LOESSER
Music by HOAGY CARMICHAEL

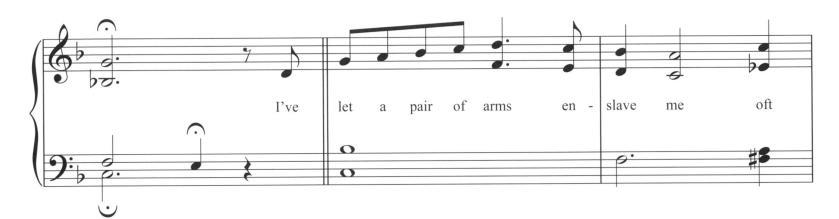

Moderately (♫ = ⌐³¬ ♩♪)

Heart and soul, _____ I fell in love with you. Heart and soul,

the way a fool would do, mad - ly, be - cause you held me

tight and stole a kiss in the night. Heart and soul, _____

_____ I begged to be a - dored. Lost con - trol and tum - bled o - ver-board

glad - ly,   that mag - ic night we   kissed   there in the

moon - mist.   Oh! but your lips were   thrill - ing,

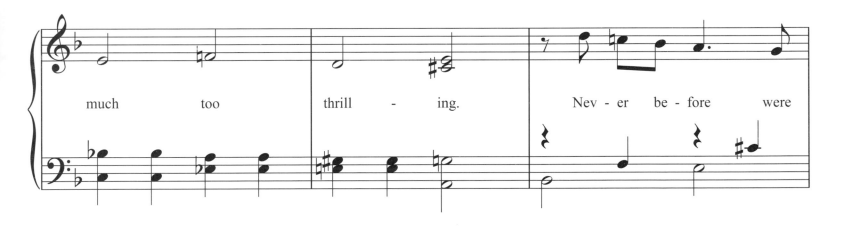

much   too   thrill - ing.   Nev - er be - fore were

mine   so   strange - ly   will - ing. But

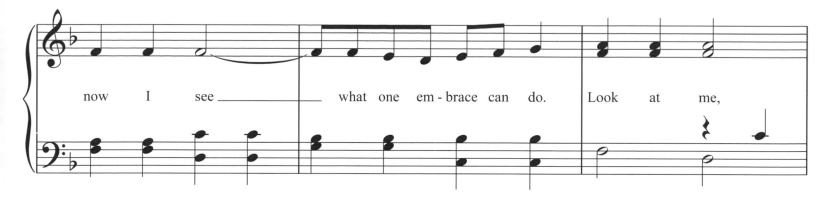

now I see ____ what one em - brace can do. Look at me,

it's got me lov - ing you mad - ly, that lit - tle kiss you

stole held all my heart and soul.

1.

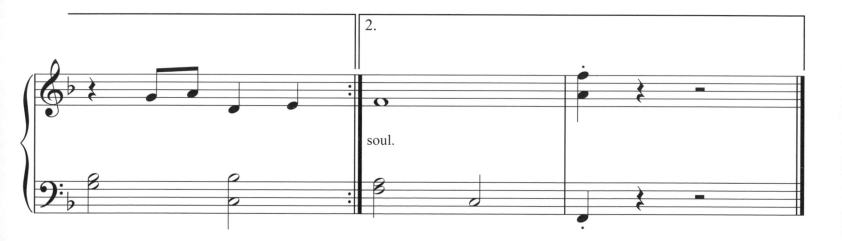

soul.

2.

I DON'T NEED ANYTHING BUT YOU
from the Musical Production ANNIE

Lyric by MARTIN CHARNIN
Music by CHARLES STROUSE

Happily

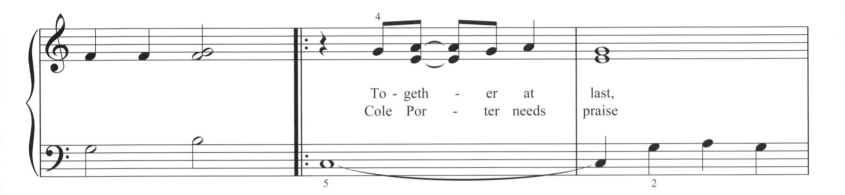

To - geth - er at last,
Cole Por - ter needs praise

to - geth - er for - ev - er;
in or - der to write more;

we're ty - ing a
Lu - go - si needs

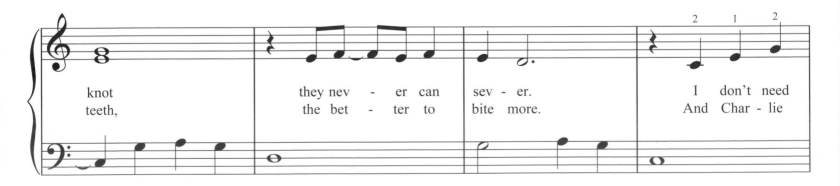

knot
teeth,

they nev - er can sev - er.
the bet - ter to bite more.

I don't need
And Char - lie

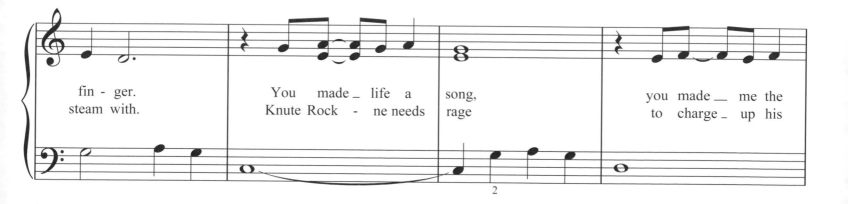

sing - er.
team with.

And what's that
And Tom - my

bath - tub tune I
Man - ville needs to

al - ways "Bub - buh -
pitch a lit - tle

boo?"
woo.

I don't need
I don't need

an - y - thing ___ but
an - y - thing ___ but

you!
you!

Yes - ter - day ___ was plain
Ham - let need - ed his

aw - ful.
moth - er,

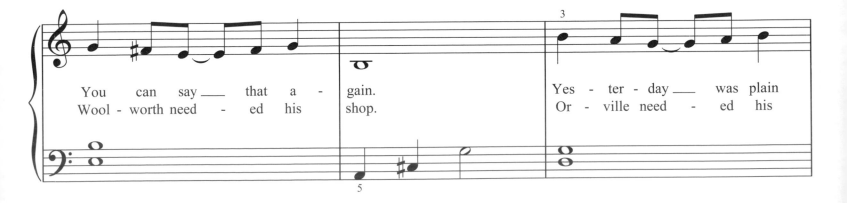

You can say ___ that a - gain.
Wool - worth need - ed his shop.

Yes - ter - day ___ was plain
Or - ville need - ed his

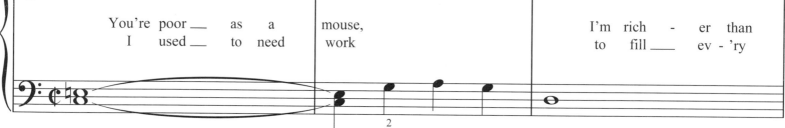

THE HOKEY POKEY

Words and Music by CHARLES P. MACAK,
TAFFT BAKER and LARRY LaPRISE

HOME SWEET HOME

Words and Music by TOMMY LEE
and NIKKI SIXX

Moderately slow

You know I'm a dream-er, but my heart's of gold. I had to

run a-way high ___ so I would-n't come home low. Just when ___

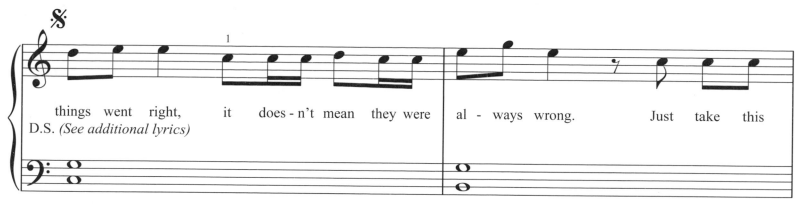

things went right, it does-n't mean they were al - ways wrong. Just take this
D.S. (See additional lyrics)

song, and you'll nev - er feel __ left all a - lone. Take me to your heart, feel me in your

bones. Just one more night, and I'm com-ing off this long and wind - ing road. __

__ I'm on my way, __ I'm on my way __ home sweet

96

home, to - night, to - night. ___ I'm on my way, ___ I'm on my

To Coda ⊕   **D.S. al Coda**

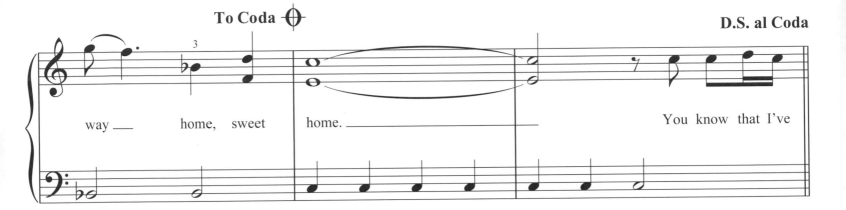

way ___ home, sweet home. ___ You know that I've

CODA
⊕

home. ___ Home sweet ___ home. ___

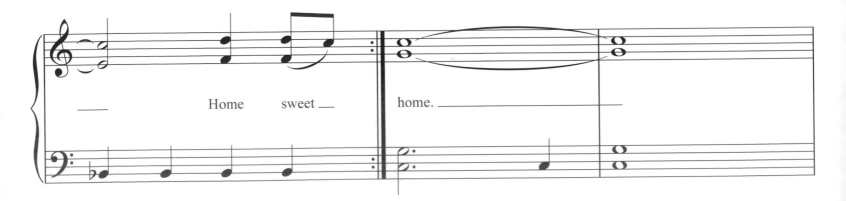

___ Home sweet ___ home. ___

Mmm, hmm, __ hmm, mmm, __ hmm, _____ mmm,

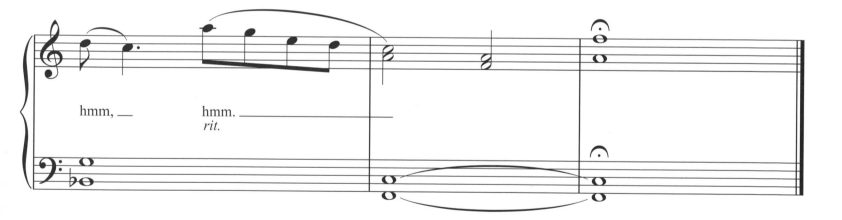

hmm, __ __ hmm. _____
rit.

Additional Lyrics

You know that I've seen too many romantic dreams
up in lights, falling off the silver screen.
My heart's like an open book for the whole world to read.
Sometimes nothing keeps me together at the seams.
I'm on my way, well, I'm on my way, home sweet home,
tonight, tonight, I'm on my way; just set me free, home, sweet home.

IF I ONLY HAD A BRAIN

from THE WIZARD OF OZ

Lyrics by E.Y. "YIP" HARBURG
Music by HAROLD ARLEN

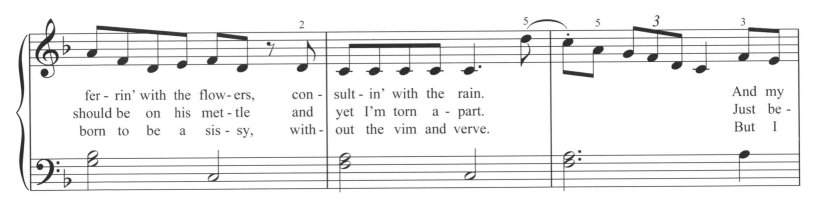

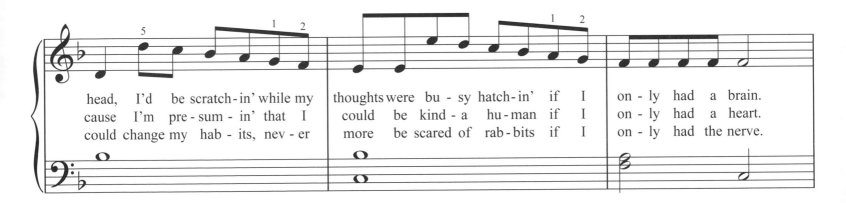

trou-ble or in pain.
gard-ing love and art.
fate I don't de-serve.

With the
I'd be
But I

thoughts I'd be think-in' I could
friends with the spar-rows and the
could show my prow-ess, be a

be an-oth-er Lin-coln, if I
boy that shoots the ar-rows, if I
li-on, not a mow-ess, if I

on-ly had a brain.
on-ly had a heart.
on-ly had the nerve.

Oh,
Pic-ture
Oh,

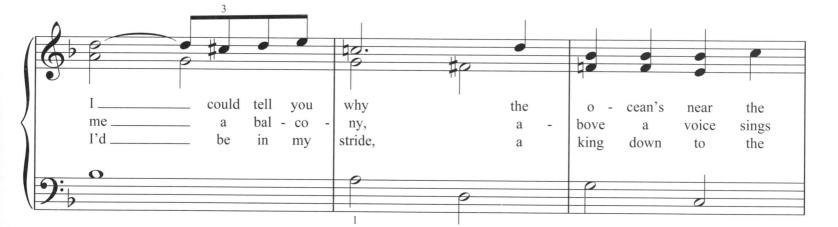

I _____ could tell you why
me _____ a bal-co-ny,
I'd _____ be in my stride,

the
a-
a

o-cean's near the
bove a voice sings
king down to the

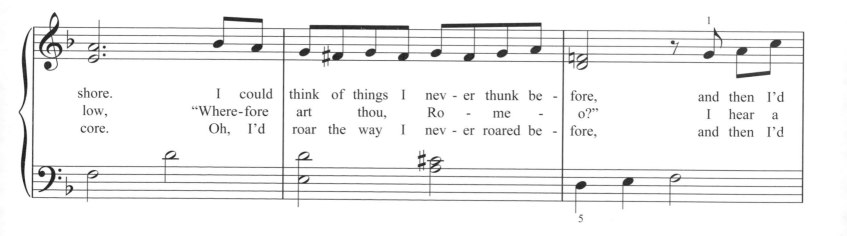

shore.
low,
core.

I could
"Where-fore
Oh, I'd

think of things I nev-er thunk be-
art thou, Ro-me-
roar the way I nev-er roared be-

fore,
o?"
fore,

and then I'd
I hear a
and then I'd

sit   and think some   more.   I would not be just a nuff-in'   my
beat.   How   sweet!   Just to reg - is - ter e - mo- tion,
rrrwoof,   and roar some   more.   I would show the di - no- sau - rus   who's

head all full of stuff- in'   my   heart all full of pain.   And per-
jeal- ous- y, de - vo- tion,   and   real - ly feel the part,   I would
king a- round the for - res',   a   king they bet - ter serve.   Why, with

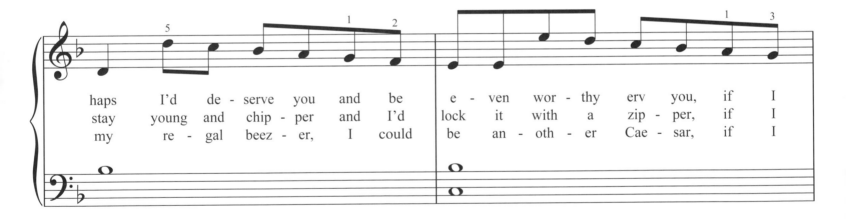

haps   I'd de - serve you and be   e - ven wor - thy erv you, if   I
stay   young and chip - per and I'd   lock it with a zip - per, if   I
my   re - gal beez - er, I could   be an - oth - er Cae - sar, if   I

1., 2.   **3.**

on - ly had a brain.   When a   Life is
on - ly had a heart.   Life is
on - ly had the nerve.

LEAN ON ME

Words and Music by
BILL WITHERS

lean ___ on. ___ I just might have a prob-lem that you'll un-der-stand. ___ We all

need some-bod-y to lean ___ on. ___ Lean on me ___ when you're not strong, ___

___ and I'll be your friend; ___ I'll help you car-ry on, ___ for it won't be long ___

___ 'til I'm gon-na need ___ some-bod-y to lean ___ on. ___

THE IMPERIAL MARCH
(Darth Vader's Theme)
from STAR WARS: THE EMPIRE STRIKES BACK

Music by JOHN WILLIAMS

8vb ⌐

IT'S A SMALL WORLD

from Disneyland Resort® and Magic Kingdom® Park

Words and Music by RICHARD M. SHERMAN
and ROBERT B. SHERMAN

Brisk March tempo

It's a world of laugh - ter, a world of
just one moon and one gold - en

tears. It's a world of hopes and a world of
sun, and a smile of means friend - ship to ev - 'ry -

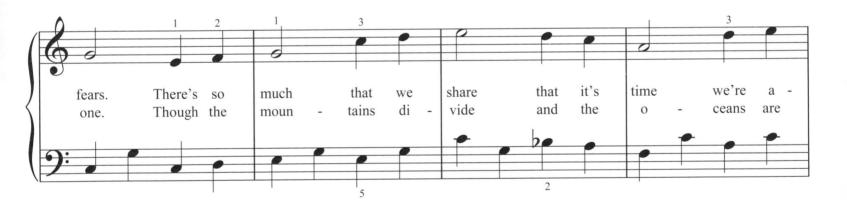

fears. There's so much that we share that it's time we're a -
one. Though the moun - tains di - vide and the o - ceans are

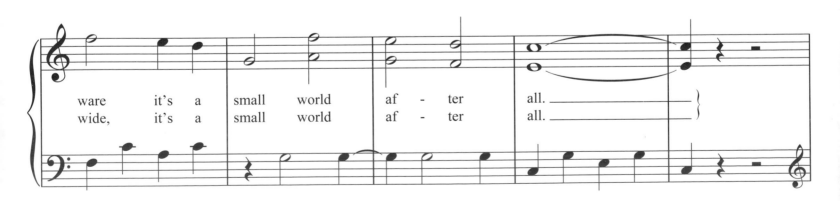

ware it's a small world af - ter all.
wide, it's a small world af - ter all.

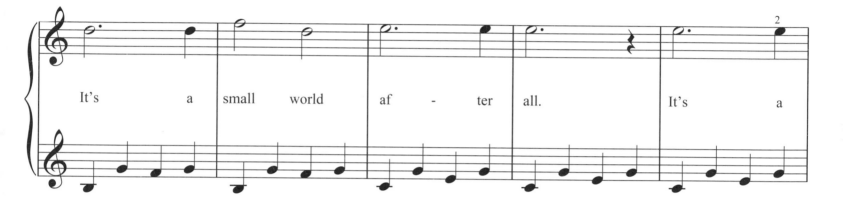

THEME FROM "JURASSIC PARK"

from the Universal Motion Picture JURASSIC PARK

Composed by
JOHN WILLIAMS

Reverently

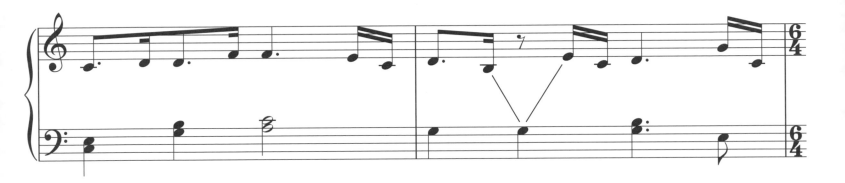

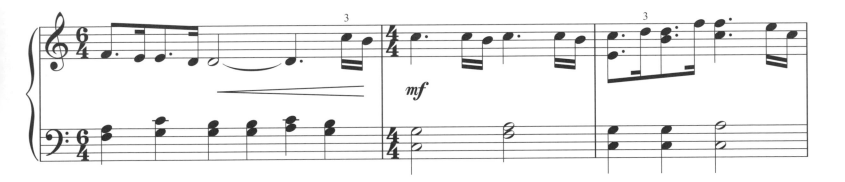

LIBERTANGO

By ASTOR PIAZZOLLA

Steady Tango

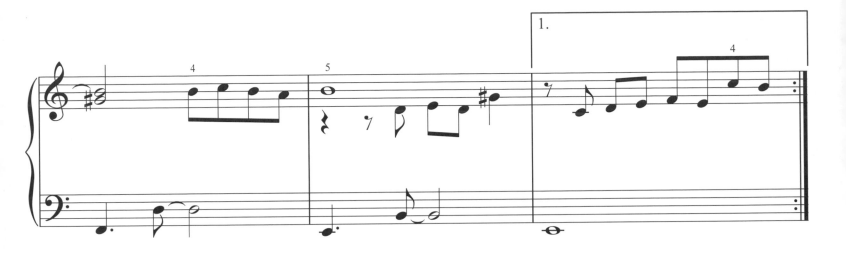

MARRIED LIFE

from Disney-Pixar's UP

By MICHAEL GIACCHINO

Moderately fast

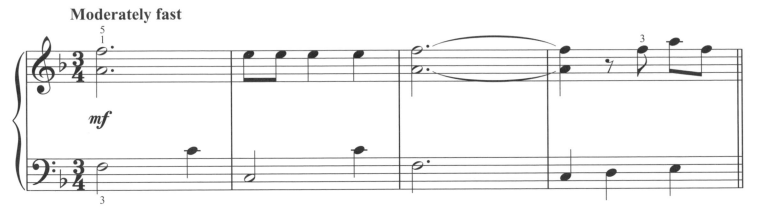

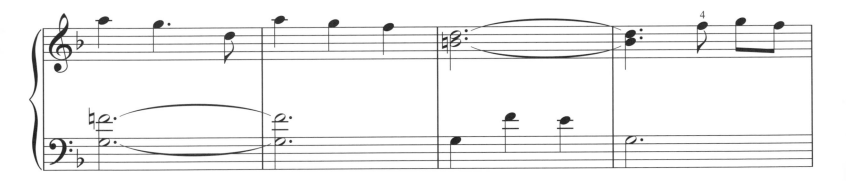

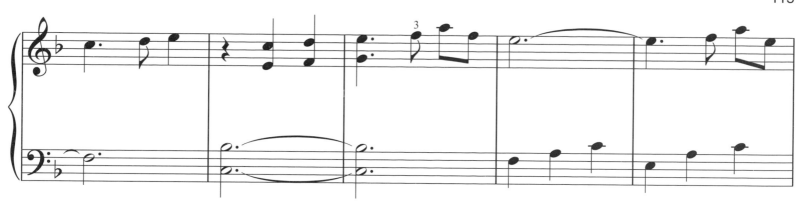

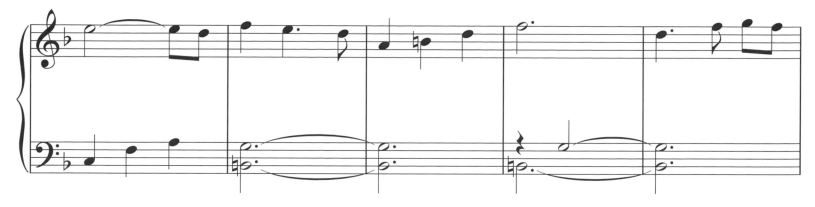

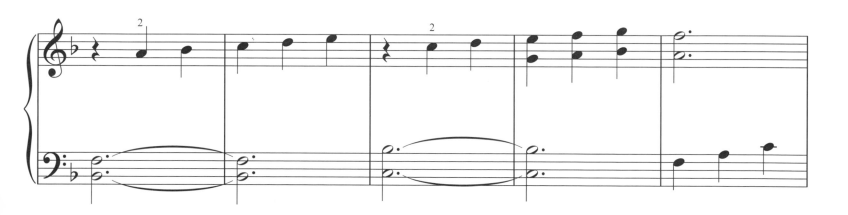

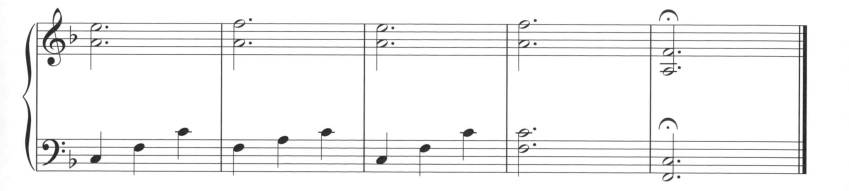

SING
from SESAME STREET

Words and Music by
JOE RAPOSO

Medium Swing

Sing!   Sing a

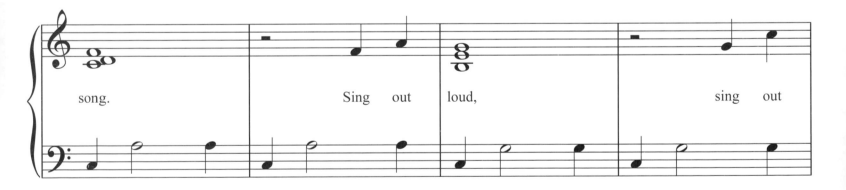

song.   Sing out   loud,   sing out

strong. _____   Sing of   good things,   not

bad. ____ Sing of hap - py not

sad. Sing! Sing a

song. Make it sim - ple to last your whole life

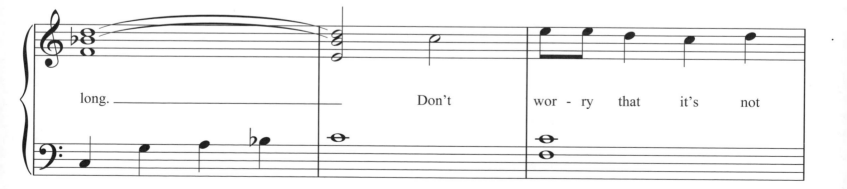

long. ____ Don't wor - ry that it's not

120

good e-nough for an-y-one else to hear. Sing! _____

_____ Sing a song. La la do la da, la

da la do la da, la da da la do la da. La la do la da, la

da la do la da, la da da la do la da.

MUSIC BOX DANCER

Composed by FRANK MILLS

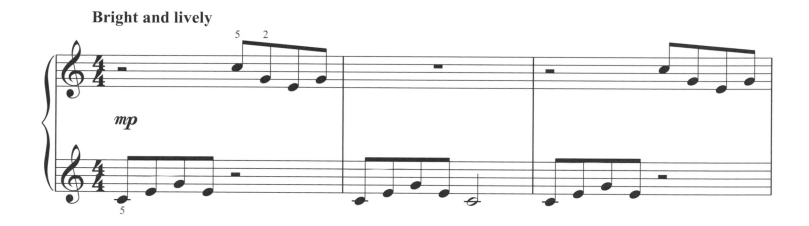

MY HEART WILL GO ON
(Love Theme from 'Titanic')
from the Paramount and Twentieth Century Fox Motion Picture TITANIC

Music by JAMES HORNER
Lyric by WILL JENNINGS

Ev - 'ry night in my dreams I see you, I

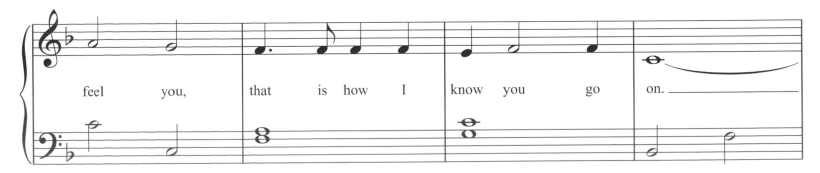

feel you, that is how I know you go on.

Far a-cross the dis - tance and spac - es be -

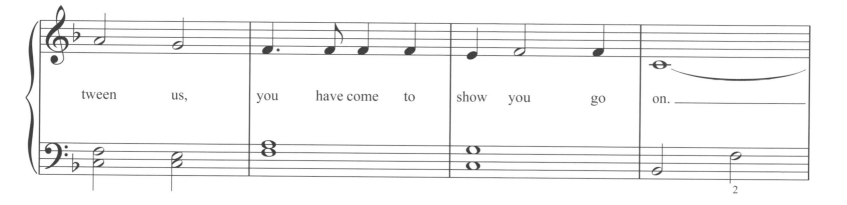

tween us, you have come to show you go on. _____

Near, far, wher - ev - er you are, _

I be - lieve that the heart does go on. _____

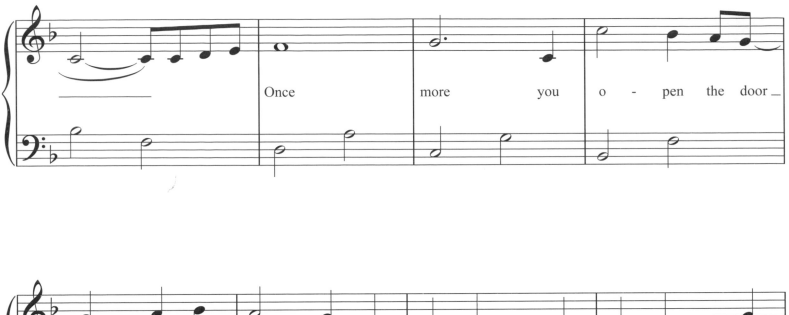

Once more you o - pen the door

and you're here in my heart, and my heart will go

To Coda ⊕

on and on.

Love can touch us one time and last for a

life - time, and nev - er let go till we're gone._____

_____ Love was when I loved you; one true time I

hold to. In my life we'll al - ways go on._____

D.S. al Coda

_____

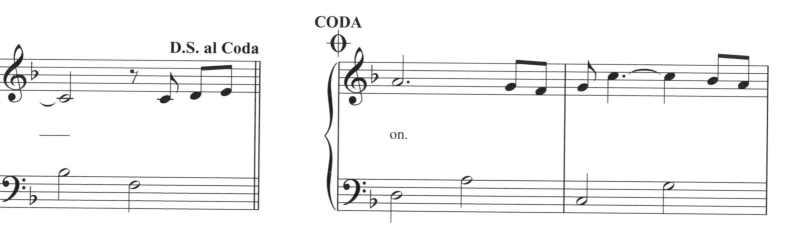

CODA

on.

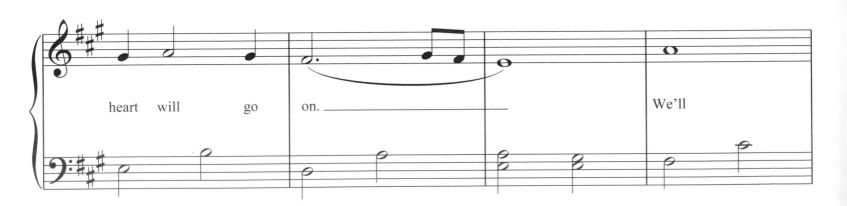

stay   for - ev - er this way.   You are safe in my

heart, and   my   heart will   go   on and   on.

dim. al fine

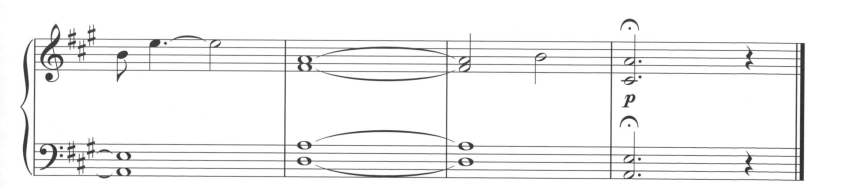

p

STAND BY ME

Words and Music by JERRY LEIBER,
MIKE STOLLER and BEN E. KING

Slowly

When the night has come and the land _____ is

dark, and the moon _____ is the on-ly light _ we'll see, _____

_____ no, I won't _ be a-fraid, no, _ I won't _ be a-

fraid _ just as long _ as you _ stand by me.

Dar - ling, stand _____ by me, won't you stand by

me. If you're in need, _ won't you stand, _ stand by me.

And if the sky that we look up - on should ev - er crum-ble and

fall, and the moun-tains _____ should fall _ to the sea, _____

no, I won't _ be a - fraid, _ no, I won't ____ shed a

tear just as long _ as you stand, _ stand by me.

Dar-ling, stand _____ by me, won't you stand by

me. If you're in need, _ won't you stand, _ stand by me.

THE PINK PANTHER

from THE PINK PANTHER

By HENRY MANCINI

Moderately, mysteriously

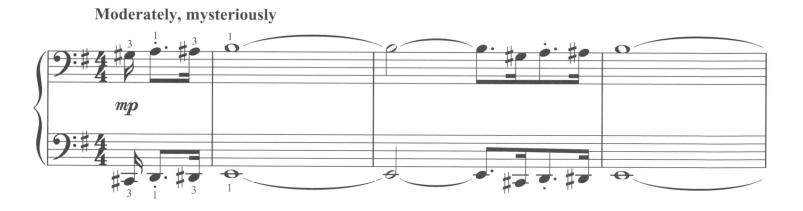

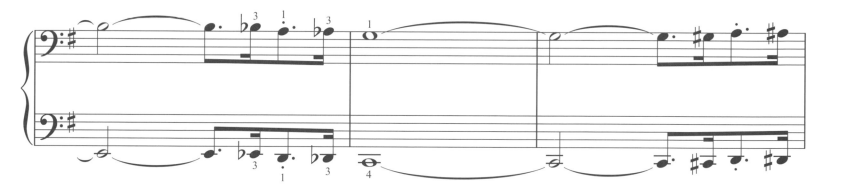

To Coda ⊕

135

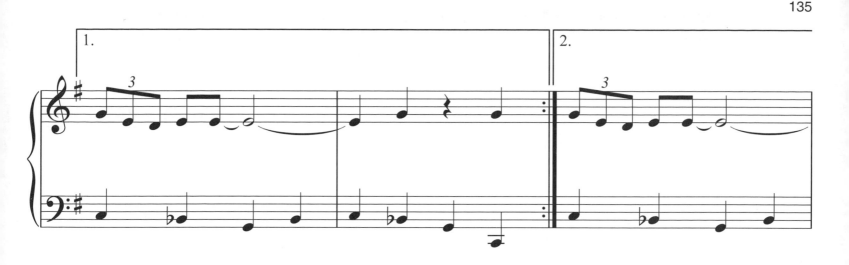

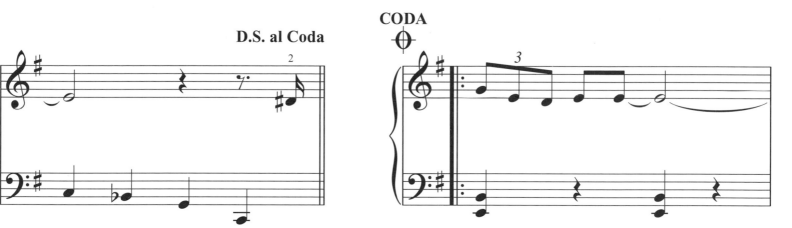

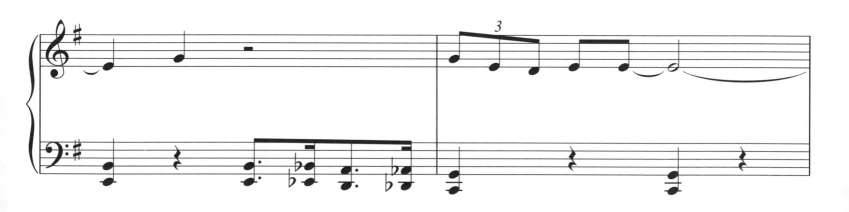

THE RAINBOW CONNECTION
from THE MUPPET MOVIE

Words and Music by PAUL WILLIAMS
and KENNETH L. ASCHER

Flowing Waltz

1. Why are there so man - y songs a - bout rain - bows, and
2. Who said that ev - 'ry wish would be heard and an - swered when
3. *(See additional lyrics)*

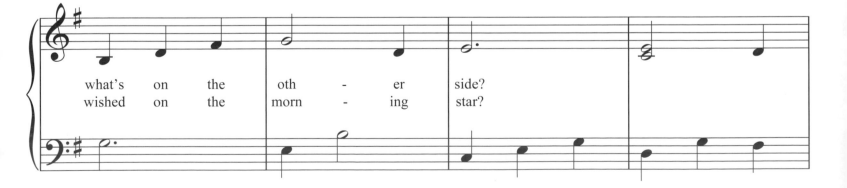

what's on the oth - er side?
wished on the morn - ing star?

Rain - bows are vi - sions, _ but on - ly il - lu - sions, and
Some - bod - y thought of that, and some - one be - lieved it;

rain - bows have noth - ing to hide.
look what it's done _____ so far.

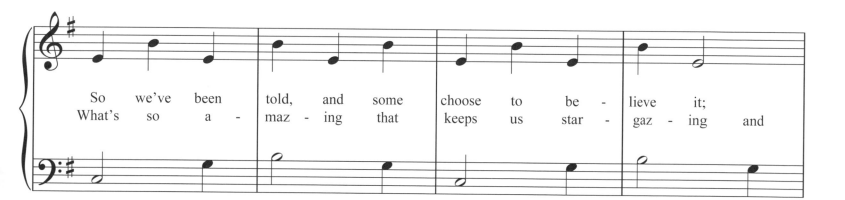

So we've been told, and some choose to be - lieve it;
What's so a - maz - ing that keeps us star - gaz - ing and

I know they're wrong; wait and see. _____
what do we think we might see? _____

Some - day we'll find it, the Rain - bow Con - nec - tion; the

To Coda

1.

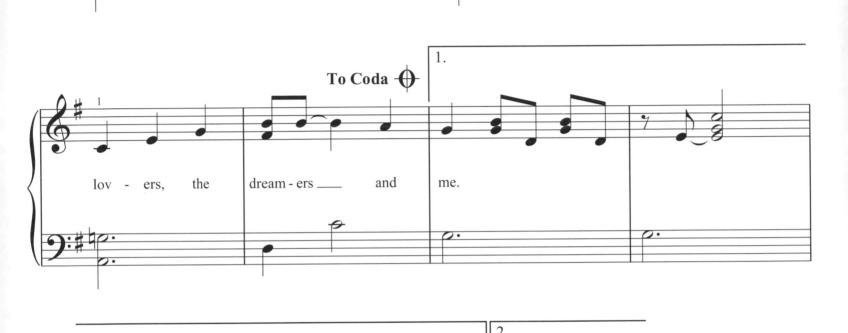

lov - ers, the dream - ers ___ and me.

2.

me. All of us

un - der its spell; we know that it's prob - a - bly

Additional Lyrics

3. Have you been half asleep and have you heard voices?
   I've heard them calling my name.
   Is this the sweet sound that calls the young sailors?
   The voice might be one and the same.
   I've heard it too many times to ignore it.
   It's something that I'm s'posed to be.
   Someday we'll find it,
   The Rainbow Connection;
   The lovers, the dreamers and me.

SKYFALL
from the Motion Picture SKYFALL

Words and Music by ADELE ADKINS
and PAUL EPWORTH

gain. _____ For this is the end. __

I've drowned and dreamt this mo - ment. _____

___ So o - ver - due __ I owe them. _____

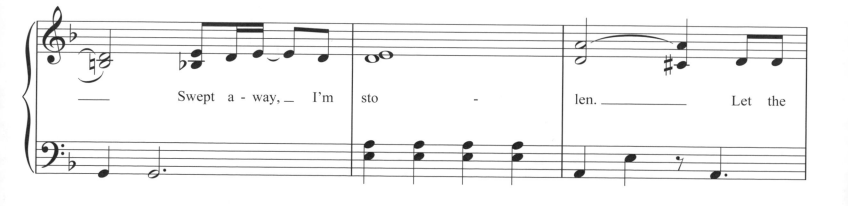

___ Swept a - way, __ I'm sto - len. _____ Let the

To Coda

a thou-sand miles and poles a-part, when worlds col-lide ___ and

days are dark. You may have my num-ber, you can take my name, but you'll nev-er have my

heart. _____ Let the

D.S. al Coda

CODA

fall. Let the sky fall. When it crum-bles,

we will stand tall. Let the sky fall. When it crum-bles,

we will stand tall.　　　Where you go,　I　go.　　What you see,

I　see.　　　I know I'll　nev - er　be　me ___ with-out the se - cu - ri - ty ___　　of your

lov - ing arms　　keep - ing　me from harm.　　Put your　hand　in　my hand　and we'll

stand. ___　Let the　sky　fall.　　When it　crum - bles,　we will　stand　tall,　　face it

all to - geth- er. Let the sky fall. When it crum- bles, we will stand tall, face it

all to - geth- er at sky - fall. Let the sky fall.

We will stand tall _____ at sky - fall, _____

ooh. _____

THE STAR-SPANGLED BANNER

Words by FRANCIS SCOTT KEY
Music by JOHN STAFFORD SMITH

Moderately, with spirit

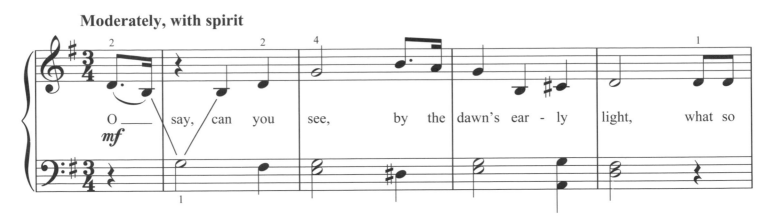

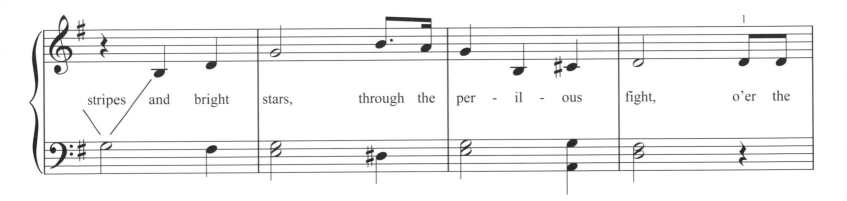

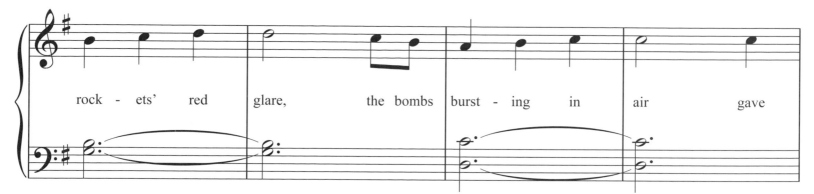

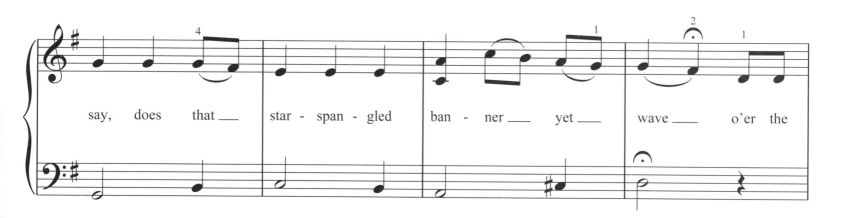

SWAY
(Quien Será)

English Words by NORMAN GIMBEL
Spanish Words and Music by PABLO BELTRAN RUIZ

Moderately

When ma - rim - ba rhy - thms

start to play, __ dance with me, __ make me sway. __

Like the la - zy o - cean hugs the shore, _ hold me close, _

sway me more. ___ Like a flow - er bend - ing

in the breeze, _ bend with me, ___ sway with ease. __

When we dance you have a way with me, ____

stay with me, ___ sway with me. ___ Oth - er danc - ers may

be on the floor, dear, but my eyes will see on - ly you.

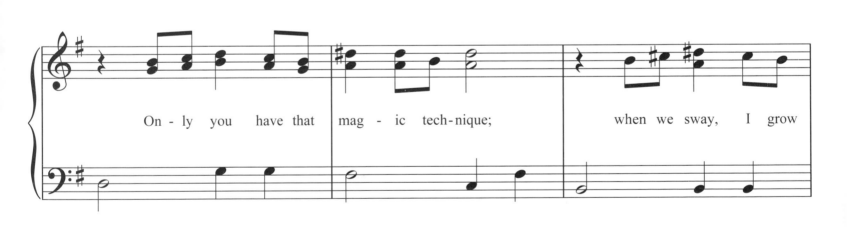

On - ly you have that mag - ic tech-nique; when we sway, I grow

weak. I can hear the sound of vi - o - lins, ___

long be - fore ___ it be - gins. ___ Make me thrill as on - ly

1.

you know how, ___ sway me smooth, ___ sway me now. ___

2.

When ma - rim - ba rhy - thms sway me now. ___

Sway me smooth, sway me now. _____

SWEET CAROLINE

Words and Music by
NEIL DIAMOND

and spring be - came the sum - mer. Who'd have be - lieved you'd come a -

long?

Hands, _____
Warm, _____

touch - in' hands, }
touch - in' warm, }

reach - in' out,

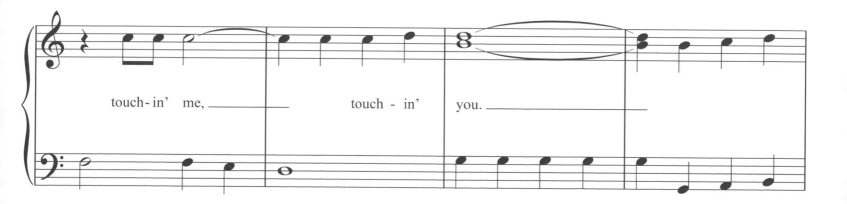

touch - in' me, _____ touch - in' you. _____

Sweet Car - o - line, _____ good times nev - er seemed so

good. _____ I've been in - clined _____

To Coda ⊕

to be - lieve _____ they nev - er would. { But now I }
{ Oh, no, no. }

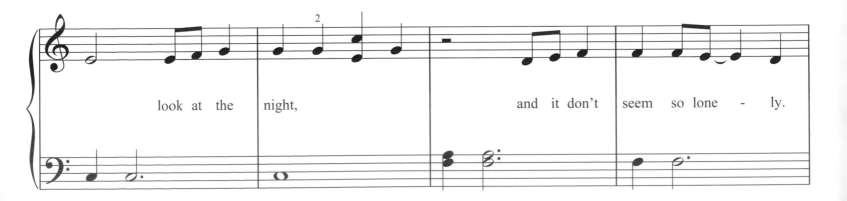

look at the night, and it don't seem so lone - ly.

We fill it up with on - ly two.

And when I hurt, hurt- in' runs off my shoul - ders.

D.S. al Coda

How can I hurt when hold - in' you?

CODA

Sweet Car - o - line, _

good times nev - er seemed so good. _____

I've been in - clined _____ to be - lieve _

they nev - er would.

TAKE ME OUT TO THE BALL GAME

Words by JACK NORWORTH
Music by ALBERT VON TILZER

Brightly

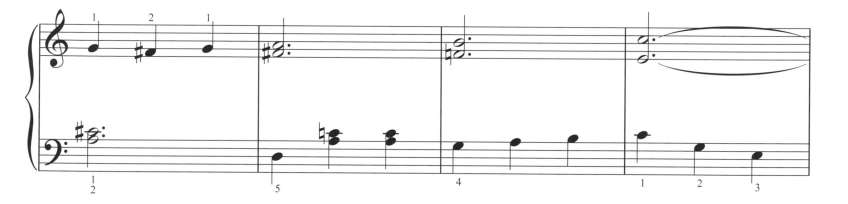

Take   me   out   to   the   ball

game, take me out with the crowd. ___

___ Buy me some pea - nuts and

Crack - er Jack; I don't care if I

nev - er get back. Let me root, root,

root   for   the   home   team,   if   they   don't

win   it's   a   shame. _____   For   it's   one,

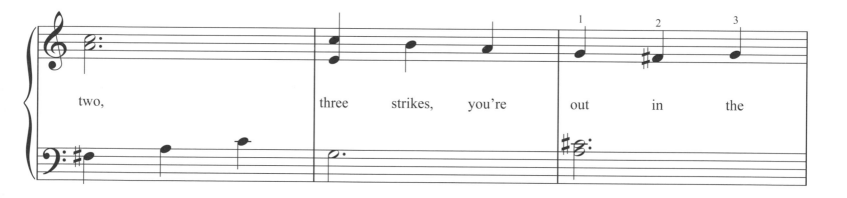

two,   three   strikes,   you're   out   in   the

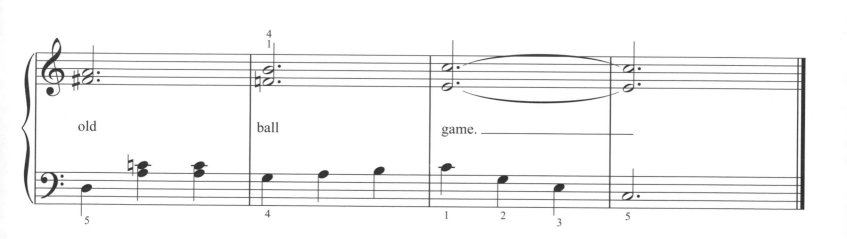

old   ball   game. _____

THIS LAND IS YOUR LAND

Words and Music by
WOODY GUTHRIE

With gusto

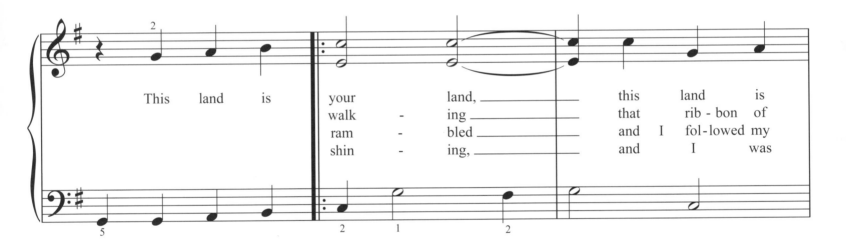

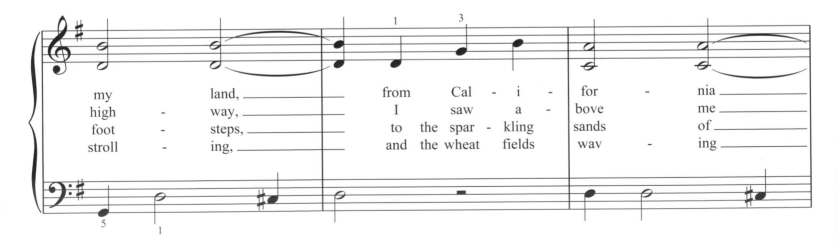

to the New York is - land, _____ from the red - wood
that end - less sky - way; _____ I saw be -
her dia - mond des - erts, _____ and all a -
and the dust clouds roll - ing, _____ as the fog was

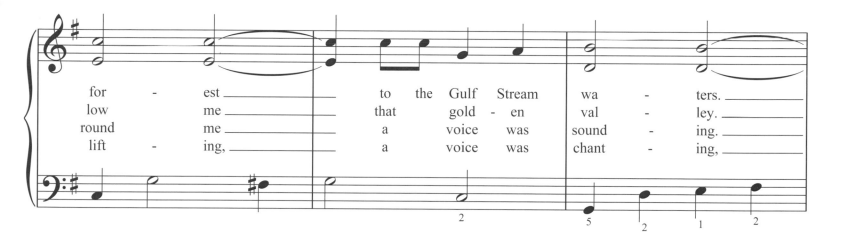

for - est _____ to the Gulf Stream wa - ters. _____
low me _____ that gold - en val - ley. _____
round me _____ a voice was sound - ing. _____
lift - ing, _____ a voice was chant - ing, _____

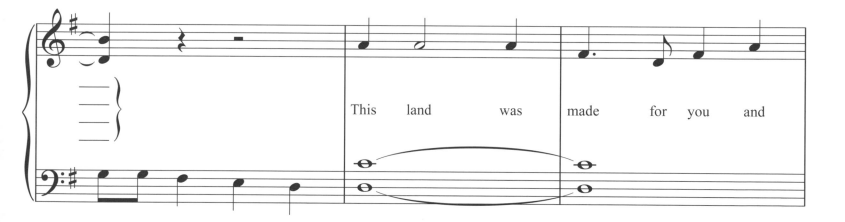

This land was made for you and

me.

As I was
I've roamed and
When the sun came

me. _____

UNCHAINED MELODY
from the Motion Picture UNCHAINED

Lyric by HY ZARET
Music by ALEX NORTH

Oh, my love, my dar - ling, I've hun - gered for your

touch a long, lone - ly time. Time goes

by so slow - ly and time can do so much. Are

you still mine? _____ I need your love, _____ I

need your love. _____ God speed your love to me.

Slightly faster

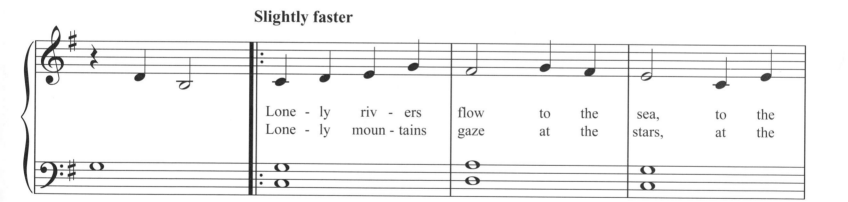

Lone - ly riv - ers flow to the sea, to the
Lone - ly moun - tains gaze at the stars, at the

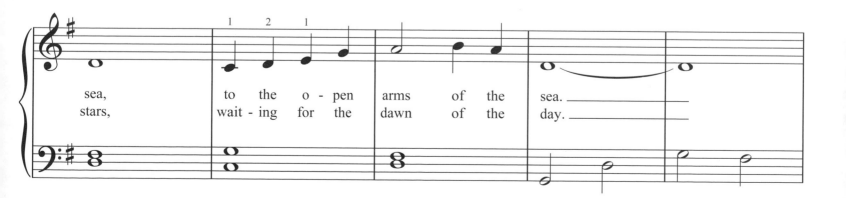

sea, to the o - pen arms of the sea. _____
stars, wait - ing for the dawn of the day. _____

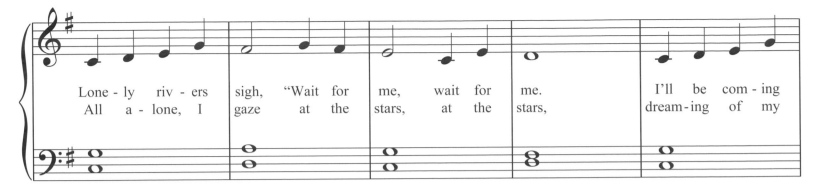

Lone - ly riv - ers sigh, "Wait for me, wait for me. I'll be com - ing
All a - lone, I gaze at the stars, at the stars, dream-ing of my

Tempo I

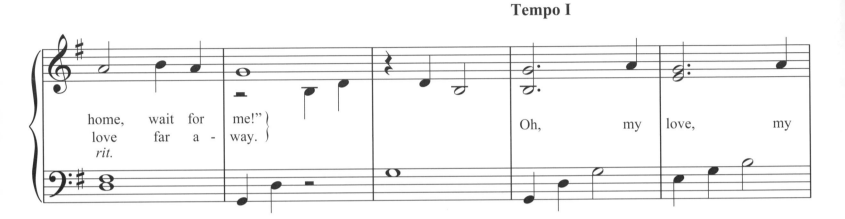

home, wait for me!" Oh, my love, my
love far a - way. *rit.*

dar - ling, I've hun - gered for your touch a long, lone - ly

time. Time goes by so slow - ly and

time can do so much.   Are   you   still   mine? _____   I

need   your   love, _____   I   need   your   love. _____   God

1.

speed   your   love   to   me.

2.

me.   *dim. e rit.*

165

YELLOW SUBMARINE

Words and Music by JOHN LENNON
and PAUL McCARTNEY

sailed _____ up to the sun till we found _____ the sea of

green, and we lived _____ be - neath the waves in our

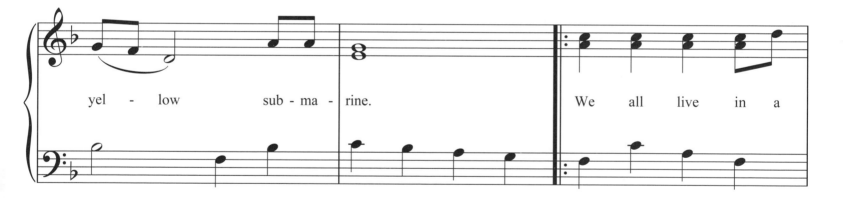

yel - low sub - ma - rine. We all live in a

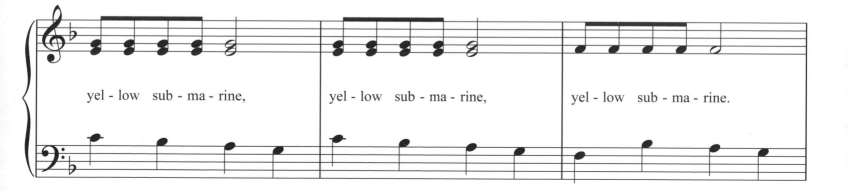

yel - low sub - ma - rine, yel - low sub - ma - rine, yel - low sub - ma - rine.

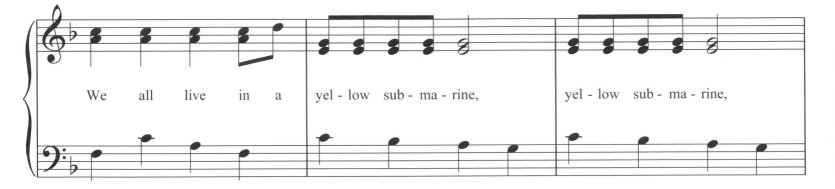

We all live in a yel - low sub - ma - rine,   yel - low sub - ma - rine,

yel - low sub - ma - rine. {And our   friends _____ are all on   board,   man - y
{As we   live _____ a life of   ease,   ev - 'ry

more of them _____ live next   door.   And the   band _____ be - gins to
one of us _____ has all we   need.   Sky of   blue _____ and sea of

1.

play:

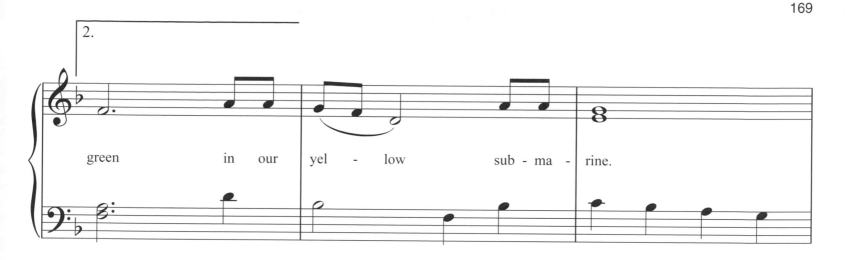

green in our yel - low sub - ma - rine.

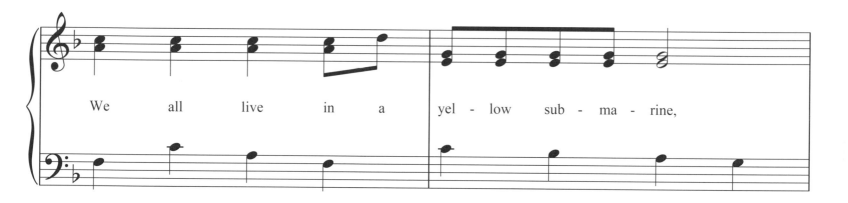

We all live in a yel - low sub - ma - rine,

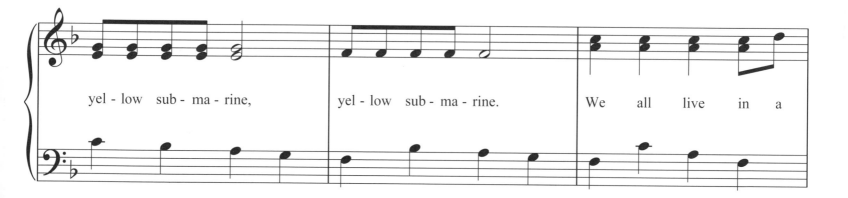

yel - low sub - ma - rine, yel - low sub - ma - rine. We all live in a

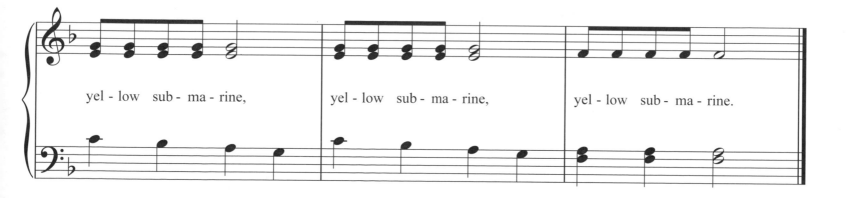

yel - low sub - ma - rine, yel - low sub - ma - rine, yel - low sub - ma - rine.

YOU RAISE ME UP

Words and Music by BRENDAN GRAHAM
and ROLF LOVLAND

Moderately slow

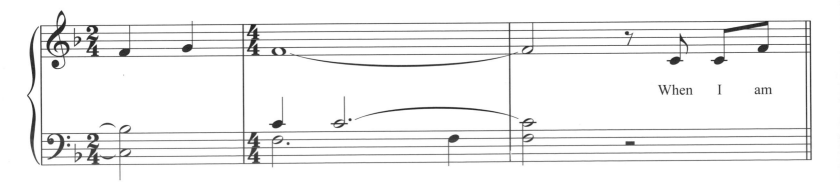

When I am

down and, oh, my soul so wea - ry, when trou - bles come and my heart bur - dened

be, then I am still and wait here in the si - lence un - til you

come and sit a while with me. You raise me up so I can stand on

moun - tains. You raise me up to walk on storm - y seas. I am

strong   when I am on your | shoul - ders.   You raise me up | to more than I can

be.

You raise me

up   so I can stand on   moun - tains.   You raise me   up   to walk on storm - y

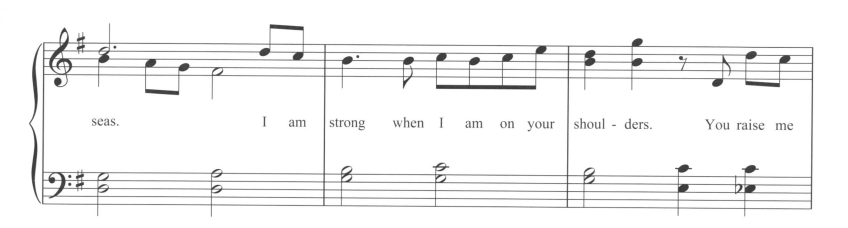

seas.   I am strong when I am on your   shoul - ders.   You raise me

up   to more than I can be.   You raise me   up   to

more   than ___ I can   be. _____

YOU ARE MY SUNSHINE

Words and Music by
JIMMIE DAVIS

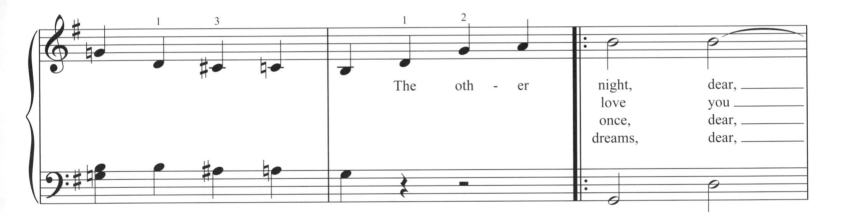

The oth - er | night, dear, _____
love you _____
once, dear, _____
dreams, dear, _____

_____ as I lay | sleep - ing _____ | I dreamed I | held you
_____ and make you | hap - py _____ | if you will | on - ly
_____ you real - ly | loved me _____ | and no | one could
_____ you seem to | leave me. | When I a - | wake my

skies   are   gray.   You'll   nev - er   know,   dear, _____

_____ how much I   love _____ you. _____   Please   don't   take   my

1.–3.   **4.**

sun - shine a - way.   I'll   al - ways
                                                    You   told   me
                                                    In   all   my